Instrument Flying

Other TAB Books by the author:

Instrument Flying

by Jeff Griffin

MODERN AVIATION SERIES

TAB BOOKS Inc.

BLUE RIDGE SUMMIT, PA. 17214

FIRST EDITION

FIFTH PRINTING

Printed in the United States of America

Reproduction or publication of the content in any manner, without express permission of the publisher, is prohibited. No liability is assumed with respect to the use of the information herein.

Copyright © 1981 by TAB BOOKS Inc.

Library of Congress Cataloging in Publication Data

Griffin, Jeff.
  Instrument flying.

  Includes index.
  1. Instrument flying. I. Title.
TL711.B6G73   629.132′52   80-28665
ISBN 0-8306-2293-4 (pbk.)

Cover photo of a 50 series Learjet with intercontinental range courtesy of Gates Learjet.

Preface

Research and photo work for this book was done over the span of an entire year, from the spring of 1979 through the spring months of 1980. The two years were as different as night and day. 1979 was stormy nearly every day in the Great Plains states. Violent weather cursed almost every flight that I made. As a matter of fact, it played an important part in my decision to change from nights to days in my flight schedule. After a complete summer of fighting nighttime giants, I was psychologically beat. When I changed, I felt that if I had to fly another belt of storms, I'd quit aviation. Of course, I wouldn't, but I sure was tempted.

This year I'm switching back to evenings. The weather just isn't as violent. Evening flying has always been the most appealing to me. It probably comes from those late nights pushing freight. Anyway, the point is that storms can be flown daily and safely. It's just that too many can make a grown man want to cry.

Another point that should be made is that weather does change from year to year. With this in mind it should be easy to draw the conclusion that some years more flights can be completed simply because there are less bad days. The converse is true and that is when we need to be prepared.

The tips in this book are intended to be a guide to completing flights on those bad days. Don't ever stick your neck out too far, yet be bold enough to learn if there is a lesson there. It may not be worth much at the time, but that lesson may pay handsome returns later.

Jeff Griffin

Acknowledgements

With every book comes a new challenge. Most times it takes a few other people to pitch in and tackle those challenges. The people at Oklahoma City Flight Service were extremely cordial and helpful. Harold Davis, one of the supervisors there, spent the better part of one afternoon shuffling me around the facility to be sure I understood everything that goes on there.

An indispensable contribution to this book was made by David Hughes of Rockwell International, Collins Avionics Division. I spent several hours long distance on the phone bending his ear on what photographs and product information I needed. Often Rockwell picked up the long distance tab. For all this I thank David, for without his help this book would not have been possible.

Last, but not least, Jim Davis of Dallas-Fort Worth Regional Approach Control lent his assistance in obtaining photographs of the radar and facility. Working hand-in-hand with these fellows daily on the airwaves, I'd like to give them credit for an excellent job at that as well.

There were too many other people to name, but I'd like to add the crews out at Ft. Sill Rapcon at Lawton, Oklahoma for their timely explanation of approach radar and procedures. Also, the guys that flew for me while I photographed deserve recognition and thanks.

Contents

Chapter 1
IFR: An Environment
With New Horizons

IFR. What is it? Well the acronym IFR represents the words *Instrument Flight Rules*. From that point the definition of IFR becomes more involved. There is nothing mysterious about IFR flying and certainly the average person would not find the subject impossible to learn. As with VFR flight (visual flight rules), there is a certain jargon that goes with this facet of flying. MEA's, MOCA's, and missed approaches seem to have ominous meanings to the neophyte instrument pilot, although the jargon is specific. All those new words are great for telling stories. Imagine yourself back at the hangar relating your last hair-raising IFR flight.

"There I was at the MDA and the RVR goes down to 1400! I didn't know whether to miss approach or cry."

The truth is that there is a brotherhood between instrument pilots. It doesn't mean that one is any better than the next guy because he can fly through clouds successfully. It *does* mean that an instrument rated pilot is better than a purely VFR rated pilot. This idea is valid to a point; it doesn't hold any water when the instrument rated pilot is not current on instruments. The great thing about the world of instrument flying is that it opens new territories to be explored (Fig. 1-1) by the individual as often as it offers a growing circle of pilot friends.

The greatest challenge in instrument flying is overcoming the fear of the unknown. It is this aspect of flying that is the most rewarding. For instance, a warm front is draped across the intended route of flight. Flying from the north side towards the front, the weather worsens and solid instrument flying becomes the standard of the day. According to the preflight briefing, there are embedded thunderstorms somewhere out there, cloaked in the gray pressing against the windshield. A tinge of fright creeps up the hairs on the back of your neck as the clouds to the right of the nose darken a little. You wonder, "Is *that* one?" The air route traffic control center confirms your suspicion. Indeed, there is precipitation being painted by ground radar. You receive a recommended vector to deviate around the darkening area. A flash of lightning splits the clouds somewhere nearby. Tightening your seat belt, you loosen your grip on the yoke and try to relax. The violent tossing and heaving could begin any second if you catch even the edge of the storm. Then suddenly, the plane pops through into brilliant sunlight and fair weather cumulus clouds. You have waged your technique and proficiency against the warm front and won. And the fear .... well, it's gone now, rinsed away by a feeling of pride and accomplishment.

It's funny how many times that instrument flight is like this. Even after thousands of hours, the feeling returns again and again for me. It is truly an on-going challenge and constant source of personal reward.

Personal challenge is not the only new horizon that opens up to the instrument pilot. An added dimension of mobility seeps into one's lifestyle. Whether you are a private pilot and fly in conjunction with your business or fly strictly to get away from it all, the ability to depart on a trip when *you* desire is the nicest thing. The sweat and money put into that instrument rating will be paid back many times in the course of your flying life. The thing a new IFR pilot should realize is that he or she is *not* ready for all sorts of minimum conditions as soon as the ink dries on the new certificate. Unless your training was much different than the average, actual IFR operations and techniques may still be quite foreign to you. There are ways to achieve experience in a safe manner and we will talk about these later. Still, the instrument rating gives almost the same reliability in completing a trip in an airplane as in the automobile.

As for the pilot who is aviation career oriented, earning that instrument rating is a giant step toward becoming a marketable commodity. Due to the new regulations which evolved in 1976, there are very few commercial pilots without instrument tickets. But, other than being able to sell your service to someone as a

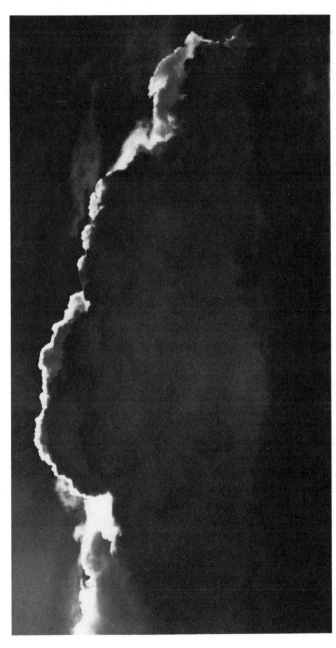

Fig. 1-1. The beauty, splendor, and grandeur belong to a relatively few people who face these awesome clouds regularly. Truly, the instrument pilot has set himself apart from the rest of mankind.

charter pilot (and other positions on up the job ladder), the IFR rating opens new horizons. You will visit places that you haven't yet heard of, like Muleshoe, Texas and Bucksnort, Tennessee. What's more, you will do it in weather in which nobody else is out!

Flying a scheduled route is interesting. Checkpoints and frequencies become well known; you learn the controllers' voices and often their names. Often these people have clues as to who is hiring and who is going bankrupt. Often one can find out where the hunting and/or fishing is the best. What has this to do with flying IFR? Nothing, except these are the things that become familiar in flying instruments often.

In addition to meeting new people and learning new things about flying, instrument flight brings other benefits. Most VFR pilots are careless and haphazard in their control of altitude. Developing a good instrument scan will carry over into a pilot's VFR flying habits. Also, the precise altitude control necessary for shooting approaches contributes significantly to all-around flying skill.

As an instructor, I always emphasized to private pilot students on their introduction to night flying that night operations were closely akin to instrument flying. For instance, when rotation takes place on a night takeoff, the nose of the aircraft will obstruct the view to the front. Horizons are difficult to discern at night. With a nose-high attitude, the problem is compounded. As a matter of course, one must then refer to the artificial horizon or attitude indicator to maintain level wings and proper climb attitude.

Night flying becomes sticky in marginal VFR conditions. In my opinion, it is *too* sticky. Before I was instrument rated I never flew in marginal conditions at night. Even now, most every night flight I make is done in the IFR environment. This way it doesn't matter if the plane punches into a deck of clouds I couldn't see ahead of time. The instrument rated pilot automatically becomes a better pilot. Even the instrument pilot who is not current (having made 6 approaches and 6 hours of flight in the last 6 months) is safer in VFR conditions at night. An inadvertant entrance into a cloud at night, though it would be surprising, probably would not tip the scales against the instrument pilot. Almost naturally, a pilot would slip into his scan. A 180 degree turn could be easily negotiated and a quick exit from the clouds made without loss of aircraft control.

From my own experience, early in my private flight training, I found that inadvertant entrance into a cloud can fluster a pilot. My instructor had always said to make a 180 degree turn and get out.

Oddly though, the use of the standard rate turn for this maneuver was not emphasized enough. I used a 30 degree bank, in a hurry to leave; 30 degrees became 45 degrees and so on. I almost achieved a graveyard spiral before I checked out of the cloud. An instrument pilot would have more snap than that.

As it goes, the instrument pilot is a better VFR pilot night and day. Many of the professional pilots I talked to on this subject remarked on how much more aware of the airplane they became after instrument training. They no longer just pointed the nose at the sky, but scanned all instruments more (Fig. 1-2). Even the engine instruments such as oil temperature, pressure and cylinder head temperatures got more attention. As a result, the pilot was more integrated into the total flying environment.

Over and over again, the pilots I chatted with remarked that the greatest thrill to flying instruments was the actual busting through clouds. The anticipation of escaping the murky gray of a rainy or snowy day is half the fun. The other half comes as the light in the tops of the clouds becomes intense and flickers of blue dance past the windscreen. Finally, the plane is suspended in bright sunshine and blue sky with a layer of the purest white below. What a privilege to have this experience and this view of the planet! The pilot is only one of a few who will see the sun in this area of the world today.

Fig. 1-2. A competent instrument pilot often finds that all instruments are checked in his scan more often, even the engine instruments.

Often, instrument flying results in a lesson in personal growth. In our everyday lives we feed our egos until we achieve a false sense of our importance. Guiding an aircraft through canyons of immense towering cumulus and thunderstorms impresses most individuals with the tremendous raw power of nature. Man, in this environment, is a fragile entity. Life often hinges on the power of decision alone. Man has no tools that can battle the awesome power of a thunderstorm. Flying next to one of these brutes tends to put life back in some sort of perspective as to our mortality. At the same time, flying through a line of thunderstorms safely and successfully yields a sense of pride that cannot be found in the remainder of our everyday lives.

Chapter 2
Get a Good Weather
Briefing

It has been said before, yet no other statement packs as much truth about IFR logic: "Instrument flying is weather flying." As an instructor, it is sad to see new private pilots have such low regard for meteorology. So many students enroll in a ground school course only to complain about having to learn weather. If you are one of those type of pilots, you *don't* belong in the IFR environment. It is extremely important that a pilot be able to "read" the weather as a flight progresses. The ability to do this comes from reading textbooks on weather (such as *Pilot's Weather Guide*, TAB book No. 2288) as well as other books such as this one. Actual flying is the other way to learn about weather, but the new instrument pilot can more safely gain the knowledge through study.

Another important piece of knowledge centers around the preflight weather briefing. If it is important to be able to "read" the weather, it is also important to be able to interpret weather reports. The Flight Service personnel invariably pass along reports and forecasts verbatim. The percentage of the Flight Service staff that has adequate knowledge of weather is definitely in the minority. The FSS personnel do take two weather courses during their training; however, application of that knowledge comes only with experience. As a result, the burden of deciding credibility of a forecast rests on the pilot. That's right; if the pilot believes the forecast is accurate *without* checking other factors, then eventually that pilot will encounter unexpected weather somewhere, someday.

The main reason that this conservative skepticism is needed is due to the weather and the weather information dissemination system. The weather is always changing. Even the blue sky on a sunny day has a limited life span. The weather charts and forecasts, on the other hand, do *not* change continually. These observations and reports come out hourly or every six or even twelve hours. The result is a great deal of information on what *has* happened and little reliable information on what *will* happen. The further a forecast reaches into the future, the greater the chance that it will be in error.

The Flight Service Station of the future as well as the National Weather Service will incorporate computer video displays that show the overall picture hourly and update any special observations as they come in. The computer will be able to extrapolate the positions of fronts and forecast their movement from data that is continually updated. The accuracy of forecasts and weather briefings to the pilot will improve substantially, especially when the pilot has access to view the computer display firsthand.

Today, the use of computers is widespread in the weather information system, yet they are not used to full advantage. Much information is available for viewing at the FSS and this is where the pilot can get the best weather briefing possible. The facsimile charts are the aids that make the difference. Being able to see these firsthand can steer a pilot towards asking the proper questions and therefore estimate the credibility of the latest forecasts. Simply put, the best weather briefings are those in which the pilot is able to visit the FSS personally.

A VISIT TO THE FSS

Flight Service Stations come in different sizes and have different size staffs. The area that the facility is located within determines the size of that facility. Houston and Oklahoma City, for instance, are large as facilities go. On the other hand, outposts such as Hobart, Oklahoma and Las Vegas, Nevada are comparatively small.

It is true that the large facilities have the more modern equipment, but the same information is available at all Flight Service Stations. That information includes facsimile charts, satellite photos, and the printed data such as hourly sequences and terminal forecasts, etc. Presently, the FSS's are in three different stages of development. The smaller stations simply have the teletyped data torn off and displayed for pilots' and briefers' use. This is the method of the past. This method has become outmoded due to the increase of pilot numbers and increased use of the airways. The airplane has become a viable competitor to the car in today's fuel-short world.

The middle stage of development which one will find at FSS's is the use of closed circuit television to aid briefers (Fig. 2-1). As many as 15 to 18 cameras are focused on facsimile charts, and each camera is assigned a channel. The briefer sitting at a panel with a TV can display a prog chart or upper winds chart, etc. to aid to briefing a pilot. In addition, there is usually a television at the front desk for pilots visiting in person (Fig. 2-2). This closed circuit television concept has essentially provided each briefer with his own set of fac charts (Fig. 2-3). In larger metropolitan areas, this method will enable the briefer to handle more pilot calls without moving to check each chart. This stage of development was hailed highly in the middle 1970's when it was first instituted in Atlanta.

The newest state of the art is the CRT (cathode ray tube) display. This a television-type computer display tied into the computer at Kansas City. The benefit of this system is that the latest weather data for any locale can be retrieved instantly after the computer has been fed the information. Also, the entire national system is available to the briefer, whereas before, each FSS was restricted to the geographical region in which it was

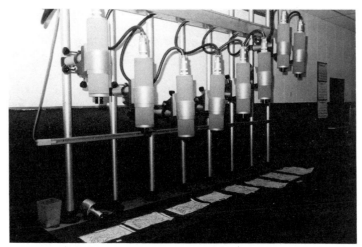

Fig. 2-1. Here, there are eight television cameras focused on various facsimile charts for display to briefers and pilots.

Fig. 2-2. This is one of the closed circuit televisions that sit at the briefer's desk. This one has 24 channels and displays the fac charts from Fig. 2-1.

located (Fig. 2-4). For instance, you fly a corporate jet out of Oklahoma City and propose a flight to Miami, Florida. The briefer will have to request the weather outside his geographical region from the computer. This may take several minutes. On the other hand, if you are departing from Denver where the new CRT displays are available, the briefer could have your route information as quickly as he can type the request into the computer. The advantage is obvious; the briefer is more efficient and can handle more pilots. On the pilot's side of the coin, briefings are quicker and more to the point. This is good when the boss shows up early and is ready to fly.

Regardless of the size and sophistication of the Flight Service Station, the weather briefing a pilot gets is dependent on the experience and background of the briefer and the questions the pilot asks. In researching this subject, Harold Davis, the shift supervisor for the Oklahoma City Flight Service Station, emphasized that the stage for the briefing is set by how much information the pilot volunteers at the outset. All the briefers I talked with reiterated this fact.

In order to handle the briefing, the briefer must know your N number and type of aircraft. The main reason for this is to confirm that he is in fact talking to a pilot. There just are not enough briefers to give the non-flying public a great deal of time. Also, in the event

Fig. 2-3. The telephone briefer has at his position all the current forecasts and hourly weather. In addition, this position is equipped with closed circuit television for viewing the fac charts.

there is ever a question as to whether a pilot received a briefing, the N number is recorded on a log.

It is just as important that the briefer know the type of aircraft you are flying. There's a vast difference between a bizjet and a

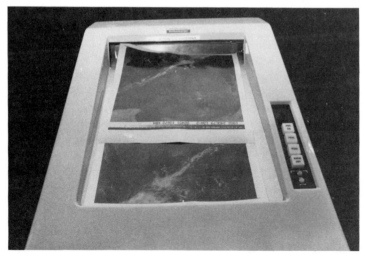

Fig. 2-4. A great way to find fronts and areas of thunderstorms is to use the satellite view. Here, the laserfax machine prints a view of the western United States.

two-seat trainer. A bizjet requires briefing on high altitude winds aloft. On the other hand, a Cessna 150 may be incapable of completing a particular mission if the low altitude winds are high. In the latter case, one could expect the briefer to give an opinion as to the feasibility and safety of the flight. We'll discuss that point thoroughly later.

One can see that volunteering just these two facts (N number and type of aircraft) answers several questions and meets the requirements of FSS protocol. Other information that a pilot should volunteer is the type of operation (IFR or VFR), the destination, and the time involved (departure time and time enroute). You may be saying to yourself, *"Time enroute?* I don't know the winds aloft. How should I know how long it will take? What do you think I'm calling for?"* Well, all the briefer would like is an estimate to the closest hour. You should say the flight will take 2-3 hours, for instance.

Taking each of these questions one at a time, let's try to understand what requirements we are filling. When the briefer is aware that a pilot can fly IFR, the briefing may be lengthy and involved; to the non-instrument-rated pilot, the briefing may be short and to the point such as, "the weather at your destination is 100 feet, sky obscured, visibility zero, and forecast to remain so. I don't think you can make your flight today."

On the other side of the coin, the recommendation to the IFR may sound different. It may be that caution is urged because the weather is below IFR minimums as well.

When the briefer knows the destination, the importance is obvious except when the destination has more than one airport. Many times a large metropolitan area has several airports. The largest of the airports usually has the best instrument approaches and minimums may often be lower for some operators.

The departure time and time enroute help the briefer fit the terminal forecast to your arrival time. The choice of an alternate is directly effected by the time period of an hour before to an hour after the estimated time of arrival.* The briefers are aware of these regulations and will normally volunteer several possible alternates for your choice.

There are specific advantages to making a personal visit to the Flight Service Station as opposed to the telephone briefing. The obvious advantage is that the pilot can see the various facsimile

---

*Revised Part 91 now requires the forecast to be known from 1 hour before to 1 hour after estimated time of arrival.

charts. If a pilot knows what he is looking for, information may be obtained by using his own knowledge that won't be brought forth in the normal weather briefing, in person or over the telephone. Wherever these advantages and disadvantages show up we will discuss them.

It is my feeling that the best way to begin a weather briefing is to review the area forecasts for your route of flight. The area forecast usually lays out general areas of cloudiness and precipitation. It also forecasts the type of precip to expect such as rain, snow, or thundershowers. Except for the prog charts, this is usually the only straightforward information given on the freezing level. In general, the area forecasts or FA's as they are known spell out the big picture in words. This is particularly handy on telephone briefings when the pilot can't study a weather depiction chart.

The only trouble with area forecasts is that the briefers don't like to read them. For some reason, most briefers think you already know this information. Obviously, the National Weather Service would not issue this information if it wasn't to be used. Thus, if a pilot requests this information the briefer must do his job.

Getting into the briefing, what comes next is not all that important. Be sure to get both current weather and terminal forecasts for the cities along your route of flight. Most all pilots and all briefers as well do this. Some of the most important information can be gained from checking the weather directly ahead of a front and immediately following a front. If a front is moving into a general area close to your destination, it is always good to learn the characteristics of this front in the event that it does not move as forecast. For instance, the front is moving faster than expected, according to an enroute weather check. At your planned arrival time the front will be just southeast of your destination. Having checked the weather prior to takeoff, you know that the weather on the backside of the front is very low IFR. At this point the wise pilot will evaluate the situation as to whether the plane's equipment and his experience level can handle the low approaches ahead.

There are a couple of other helpful hints to locating major weather disturbances that will greatly affect flight. Basically, a pilot's two great fears are ice and thunderstorms. Naturally, thunderstorms and ice are often found in the various forecast data a briefer will give you. Experience has shown me that the northeast corner of a low is the most intense in the winter and therefore can be expected to have the most moisture, precipitation, and ice.

Fig. 2-5. One of the little used methods for receiving weather information is PATWAS and TWEB. Both are recorded by the FSS specialist in this room. Recordings go out over VORs and NDBs as well as via telephones in the left of the picture.

In the spring, a young pilot's fancy turns to thunderstorm avoidance. A sure-fire combination that brings on the worst of nature is a staggered low pressure system. When a low pressure system is on the surface and an upper low is following about 150 to 200 miles to the west, the stage is set for fireworks. Such a situation existed the day that Witchita Falls, Texas was devastated by a tornado in the spring of 1979. As a pilot, to uncover this situation one must look at the 500 mb and 300 mb charts for the upper low to the west. A personal visit to the FSS makes these conditions easy to examine. However, over the phone, pointed questions must be asked. Where is the low pressure system centered now? Sounds like you are being picky? Just remember, it is *your* butt up there trying to fly that weather, *not* that joker on the telephone.

Another chart that is nice to check when visiting in person is the airmass stability chart. These aren't found at every FSS, but can help. The areas on the map along fronts and pressure systems are accompanied by fraction representation. The top number is the lighted index and the bottom number is the K index. These indices are figured by equation and are not important to us. What is important is that when the top number in the fraction has a negative value and the bottom is positive, the chance for thunderstorm activity is high.

Being able to get a briefing at the Flight Service Station first hand has obvious advantages in picking alternates. First of all, one can view the surface weather depiction chart. This is the chart that has the scalloped lines for marginal VFR and the solid lines for IFR. By glancing at this chart a pilot can see the areas of IFR and how extensive they are. If there is an area of marginal VFR near your destination, that would be the likely area to shop for an alternate.

The briefing over the phone poses a special problem. The pilot does not have a weather depiction chart to help in requesting an obvious alternate. In this respect the FSS briefer can help you if you furnish him the fuel radius of the aircraft you're flying. For example, with the load you intend to carry, the plane will fly an additional one hour and a half. That must include the 45 minute IFR reserve, thus the time to the alternate cannot exceed 45 minutes. Depending on the speed of the plane that is being flown, a radius of operation can be estimated. The briefer armed with this information looks for an alternate within the restricted radius. Of course, a pilot may request the weather at a prospective alternate if he favors that airport. However, if your favorite alternates are socked-in, then searching for an alternate becomes trial and error and it is best to give the briefer your fuel radius.

USING FLIGHT WATCH

I am not convinced that the Enroute Advisory Flight Watch program has added another dimension to the Flight Service Station

Fig. 2-6. Won't someone give this man something to do? This is the Flight Watch position as well as other standard Flight Service radio frequencies. It is a help to your fellow pilots when you make PIREPs.

(Figs. 2-5, 2-6). It seems the old 122.2 did the same work and worked well. The Flight Watch frequency is 122.0. The one thing that *has* improved (but not greatly) is the availability of pilot reports. Flight Watch actually solicits pilots to make reports. This helps tremendously when various weather phenomena are occurring between reporting points. It's nice to know that VFR cannot be maintained between points A and B when they are both reporting "clear and a million."

The best use of Flight Watch is when conditions are changing fast or might change quickly. In the winter, especially across the snow belt, fog becomes a problem at night. Many times, warmer air will move in over the snow cover and cause fog. A briefing before takeoff might indicate a small temperature-dewpoint spread. This should alarm a pilot sufficiently to warrant enroute weather checks. If fog is expected, weather reports may be issued more often that every hour as the visibility deteriorates. In a case such as this, calls to Flight Watch about every 20 minutes are a good idea. Many times I've undertaken a one hour flight where the destination was holding 3 miles visibility, but showing lower. Frequent checks ahead confirmed our suspicions. At the arrival the visibility was down to a half mile. The approach was a tight one.

As a professional pilot, I use Flight Watch often to make pilot reports. So many times other pilots are forced to stay on the ground in the winter, for instance, because icing conditions are forecast. Many times those forecasts are incorrect, but without a pilot report no one will ever know it! That is why a pro should make pilot reports. There are a lot of other pilots sitting on the ground without anti-ice and de-ice protection who could be flying if they knew the true conditions.

Essentially, it is every pilot's responsibility to report deteriorating conditions and warn others. If all of us made these pireps when they were called for, the overall weather picture would be improved in every pilot's mind. The instrument pilot often has a vantage point that the VFR bound pilot does not. If you can recall how it was when you were a VFR pilot, not knowing whether the weather was good enough to make the flight outside of instrument conditions, then the empathy should be there. The instrument pilot many times departs uncontrolled airports at outposts that have no weather reporting. Reporting the clouds bases as one departs an area will help our VFR brothers as well as other IFR flights inbound to the same airport.

Pilot reports are part of the substance of the brotherhood of flying, pilots looking out for pilots. Whether they are made to Flight Watch directly or to ATC they may save the bending of an airplane somewhere. In the following chapter we will discuss ATC type pilot reports.

RADAR SUMMARIES

Checking the radar summary during a weather briefing is a wise thing to do. The problem with radar summaries is the ease in which they become outdated. The facsimile chart that comes off of the facs machine is outdated as soon as it hits the briefer's hand. The reason: the information is fed into the computer at Kansas City, then the printing of that chart takes several minutes.

Some of the Flight Service Stations have a radar monitor which is a repeater of a National Weather Service unit. Many times the monitor is available to pilots who visit in person. Briefings over the telephone are enhanced by the availability of the repeater to the briefer.

Early in April 1979, the radar repeater played a large part in my "go-no go" decision. The television was on at the airport and the TV weatherman was talking about some storms that were developing out to the west of us. We were in Lawton, Oklahoma. A call to the Flight Service Station revealed only a chance for thunderstorm development during the afternoon and evening. I asked the briefer then to check his radar because I had heard of some developing cells to the west. His response was that was the first he had heard of them and would take a look. He returned in a minute or two and said *yes*, there were some and they seemed to be clustering.

"If they continue to build and move in the direction they are moving we may get some of it before the evening is through."

I checked the radar installations at Altus Air Force Base and the Fort Sill Army installation. The reports grew more ominous as the minutes passed. The storms were lining up, clustering and growing taller. I elected to sit tight. Within an hour the area between Witchita Falls and Lawton was saturated with tornados and flying debris. Indeed, the briefer was right: Wichita Falls did get some of it as 43 people died and thousands lost their homes and possessions.

As you can see, the radar picture (especially in spring and summer) is extremely important. If the FSS does not have a repeater from a radar installation, then the radar summary chart is the next best thing. Unfortunately, the radar summary is always outdated. Another thing: just because one lives in an area where violent weather is rare, a check should be made for safety's sake.

A WORD ABOUT NOTAMS

Notices to Airmen (Notams) are often neglected in the preflight briefing. The reason for this can be blamed on both sides. The pilot may think to himself or herself that he has recently flown the same route and knows the situation. If fact, a VOR may have malfunctioned, or the airport authority has decided to repave the only hard surfaced runway that has an instrument approach. The briefers are guilty as well because, having given the information to several pilots that day, they feel like they have given that information to *everybody*.

The sort of information in Notams are changes in frequencies, hazards near an airport or runways, and the malfunction of navigational aids. I remember seeing a pilot enter a traffic pattern at a busy general aviation airport and given light signals to land. He had a radio and it was working—on the *old* tower frequency. He hadn't checked the Notams before leaving his departure point. The incident was forgotten but did cause a strain on the controllers and embarassment for the pilot. The message is clear. We really ought to ask for Notams and not expect the briefer to volunteer them because they are as human as you and I.

THE WRAP-UP

In order to get the best briefing possible the pilot ought to do these five things.

1. Tell the briefer you are a pilot. If you are a student, private, or a commercial pilot tell him so. Knowing your level of skill helps.

2. Name the type of airplane you are flying.

3. Name your destination and any unusual deviations from the straight line flight path. Also, let them know if you intend to stop enroute.

4. Volunteer your departure time and estimated time enroute.

5. Tell the briefer whether or not you can go IFR. Many times, being instrument rated is not enough. Often, the weather calls for an experienced instrument pilot, not a newly rated or a non-current one.

Here's a final list of the necessary information a pilot should obtain in a preflight weather briefing:

1. Weather synopsis (position of lows, fronts, ridges etc.)
2. Current weather conditions.
3. Forecast weather conditions.
4. Alternate routes (if neccessary).
5. Hazardous weather.
6. Forecast winds aloft.
7. Notam information.

All of these items are on the briefer's checklist. However, some briefers skip over or only lightly touch on some of these items. In that case, it is up to the pilot to make sure he receives *all* the pertinent weather and notam data. The pilot is the final authority and is responsible for all flight operations. That regulation begins with and includes the preflight weather briefing.

Chapter 3
ATC and the IFR
Environment

It occurred to me one day that flying IFR was actually the combination of two environs. Plugging along in the soup, solid on the gauges, the world shrinks to the size of the airplane itself. Thick clouds bring the gray right down to the windshield and the wingtips are as fuzzy as if they were miles away. Inside, the drone of the engine and the hiss of the wind are the only hints that this transition through space is not surreal; the only hints, that is, except the crackle of the radio. The commands over the radio and the necessity of the pilot to navigate his plane over horizonless miles from the complete IFR environment.

It is easy, at least in relative terms, to control an aircraft by reference to instruments. The flight instructor worth his salt makes learning instrument flight enjoyable and fairly effortless. Again, we are only talking about flying by reference to the flight instruments. The part of instrument flying that lacks the most instruction is dealing with ATC. This is not the fault of any instructor. There is just not the time in the average instrument rating curriculum for the student to experience the many phases of instrument flight. Herein, lies a good reason why a newly certificated instrument pilot is not fully prepared to deal with the instrument environment. (For a full discussion of ATC, see *How The Air Traffic Control System Works*, TAB Book No. 2262.)

Experience is the best teacher, but there are things that can be learned from reading and that is the purpose of this book. Radio communications are a critical link in the Air Traffic Control system (Fig. 3-1). The radio link can be a strong bond between the

Fig. 3-1. The radio link can be a strong bond between the controller and pilot, but the bond can be broken instantly, sometimes with disastrous results. Here, in the subdued light of the control room, a controller handles arrivals from the west into DFW regional airport.

controller and pilot, but the bond can be broken instantly, sometimes with disastrous results. The following discussion should help the instrument pilot to fit smoothly into the system.

RADIO COMMUNICATION

The greatest sin new pilots commit in the IFR system is to over-talk. *Clarity* and *brevity* are the commodities most appreciated

Fig. 3-2. Be sure to acknowledge the frequency change when being handed off to the next sector (courtesy of Piper Aircraft Corp.).

by controllers and professional pilots. On this point, one does not have to fly for a living in order to possess a professional attitude.

Take this conversation, for example, between a pilot and Regional Approach Control at Dallas.

Pilot: Dallas-Fort Worth Regional Approach, this is Mooney 201 Mike at 5,000 feet with information Echo.

Controller: Mooney 201 Mike depart Boids (intersection), 100 degrees.

Pilot: Roger, 201 Mike when we get to Boids we'll turn to 100 degrees.

The pilot in this case was not nearly as bad as some I've heard. Yet, the conversation could be shortened immensely by using just key words and phrases. Let's clean up the conversation the way it should be.

Pilot: Regional Approach, Mooney 201 Mike, 5,000 with *Echo*.
Controller: Mooney 201 Mike, depart Boids, 100 degrees.
Pilot: 100 degrees after Boids, 201 Mike.

I swear sometimes some pilots sound like they're going to give the controller their life stories, blood types and mother-in-law's maiden name. Key words, such as 5,000 with Echo takes care of a great deal. It is obvious that 5,000 means 5,000 feet and Echo is the current ATIS information for the airport of intended landing. In areas such as Chicago, Dallas, and large cities in general there are several IFR equipped airports with ATIS tapes. Some pilots specify the airport with the ATIS identification such as ". . . with Victor Love" or ". . . Midway Charlie." This only adds one word to the conversation and may serve to keep the controller straight on how to handle your arrival. However, the controller does have a "strip" on each flight with your flight plan and need only consult it. Flying professionally, especially under a company name such as Great Western, Federal Express, Air Ohio or even American and Eastern, the controller automatically sorts the name with the usual airport of use. In this case, it is unusual to hear a scheduled carrier say ". . . Foxtrot Regional."

The newly rated pilot can learn a great deal from listening to the crews of scheduled carriers. Ordinarily, their radio manners are impeccable. For instance, it is considered good etiquette to read back a clearance and to read it back in the order in which it was given. Also, notice that in the corrected conversation of the Mooney pilot above, that he finishes his transmission with his call sign. This is common to the scheduled air carriers. The reason it is

This is particularly true in the event of transmitter failure in the aircraft. In other words, the controller can be received, but only transmitted to by identing or squawking stand-by. Many ATC facilities are now equipped with ARTS III radar which reads the transponder code being squawked. The changing of the code can also be accepted as a perfectly good radio transmission. However, recently I talked to some controllers about this and they indicated that this was not very satisfactory. Due to the fact that it takes at least two radar sweeps for the computer to read a transponder code, there is a time lapse. Several seconds will go by before the new code is posted. A controller who is very busy may not notice the change for quite a while. Therefore, it is best to read back the new transponder code and not wait for the computer to inform the controller whether we got the code correct or not. It is courteous and may speed up the handoff to the next sector for all parties concerned.

In the same vein of things are acknowledgement of frequency changes (Fig. 3-2). When you acknowledge a frequency change, you cover two questions in the controller's mind. One, the controller knows that you have received the proper frequency of the next sector. Second, if you say nothing and change the frequency, the controller has no way of knowing whether you changed frequencies or have lost radio communication. For the controller whose area one is leaving, the workload is increased. He must now make a telephone call to the next sector to verify if you came across. Although most of us don't feel too badly about working the controller a little harder, the discourtesy may interfere with the quality of service others are receiving after we changed frequencies. The controller after all cannot be calling out conflicting traffic if he is talking to another controller on the land line to find out what happened to us. So, let's not just think of ourselves or be lazy. Flying is a brotherhood and we should look out for our brothers.

ATC RADAR

ATC's radar facilities come in different shapes and sizes. The trend, however, is towards computerized data blocks and computer enhanced target displays. The days of the broadband, raw data display are coming to a close. In many ways, the broadband equipment was superior to the new installations. That is, information to the pilot was of a higher grade. Well, that isn't *exactly* true. A truer statement would be that the new ART III type arrangement does more things than the old, but directly depends on how much the controller wants to twiddle the knobs to help a pilot.

There are two major differences between broadband displays and computerized displays. The broadband radars showed areas of precipitation more readily than says, ARTS III, for example. On the other hand, ART III shows the various altitudes of encoder equipped aircraft (Fig. 3-3). So we can see on the one hand, broadband radar will help a controller describe weather areas to a pilot, but ARTS III will be more useful in pointing out conflicting air traffic. It is easy to understand that we deal with conflicting air traffic on a minute to minute basis, but turbulent weather is rare per hour of flight. Hence, the reason that the move is towards computerization.

Since, computer displays of air traffic are designed to eliminate anomalous propagation and weather, the pilot needs to understand the systems in order to get more use of the information. To say it another way, the pilot who is informed about computerized systems is able to ask intelligent questions of the controller. The result is that more flights are completed and air traffic controllers are more willing to volunteer information.

We should start by discussing some of the innovations that make radar more usable to follow air traffic. There are two main accessories to most traffic radar installations. They are the Moving Target Indicator or M.T.I., and circular polarization. MTI is circuit that limits what the radar receiver will paint on the cathode ray tube or screen. Essentially, the MTI circuit was invented and designed to eliminate ground clutter. It does this job very well. The MTI can be set for a specific speed, one mile per hour, for example. Any target that is not moving at least one mile per hour is automatically eliminated from the radar display. Things such as tall buildings, television antennas or mountains are not displayed.

The speed that is selected on the Moving Target Indicator depends on the type of traffic each particular radar facility handles. The approach controls that move a great deal of jet traffic may have their MTI set as high as five miles per hour. Similarly, a radar facility that works with slower traffic such as helicopters may have the MTI set very low. Fort Sill Radar Approach Control at Lawton, Oklahoma is such an operation. Fort Sill is an army base with many helicopter movements each day. Oklahoma is famous for its high winds and on those windy days a helicopter on landing approach has a ground speed that is nil. In these instances, the moving target indicator must necessarily be set low.

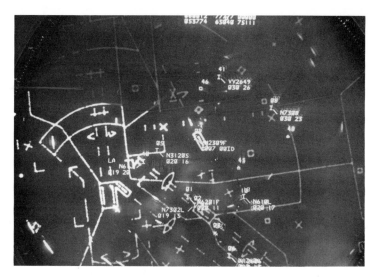

Fig. 3-3. This is the ARTS III radar used by Dallas-Fort Worth approach. The numbers are computer-generated alphanumerics. The "I" represents an identified target. Each aircraft has three numbers in its data block, the N number and two more below it. The left number is the altitude. The right number is the groundspeed with the last zero dropped. Also, the transponder can be displayed at the touch of a button.

As far as weather painting ability being hindered by the MTI: it is bothered very little. Only those showers that are stationary or nearly so will be eliminated by the circuit. So, essentially the MTI limits clutter but circular polarization will eliminate weather returns.

Circular polarization was designed to aid in tracking targets through areas of weather. What circular polarization means is that the radar signal is transmitted in a rotary fashion. The normal fashion for radar signals to be transmitted is straight out and straight back. The trouble with this is that everything is reflected back that has the ability to reflect. With circular polarization only strong targets tend to be returned. Understand that precipitation is not eliminated completely. More than likely, just the heaviest precip areas will be shown. Moreover, the circular polarization distorts the shape of the precipitation area. This fact is most important because it directly affects the information that the controller gives us.

It was early November when I came face to face with an irate line of thunderstorms. Traveling north out of Dallas towards Lawton, Oklahoma, we first went north towards Ardmore. The lightning could be seen for a hundred miles ahead of the storms. As we approached the line it looked as though we could stay VFR below them and shoot some gaps that were painting on our airborne radar. It was about this time that we started working with the controller, *intimately*. The situation, as far as flying through thunderstorms, was the best a pilot could hope for. We had airborne radar, ground radar, and best of all fairly high cloud bases. The line of storms was arranged in the typical southwest to northwest fashion. We proceeded west to step inside a hole with a turn to the north. As we stepped through the hole all hell broke loose. The visibility remained good with only light rain but the turbulence was about to take the plane apart. In a mile or two the turbulence subsided to a more tolerable level, but still moderate in intensity. Inside the front line of storms we found a surprise: *another* line of storms. This one was solid with no visible holes on our airborne radar. ATC was saying that the line way only ten miles wide in one certain area, but *our* radar was showing that it was more like 20 miles and solid. We were on vectors now with lightning flashing all around.

I knew the voice of the controller as a friend of mine. He was being very professional, but it is obvious in retrospect that a controller is under a great deal of pressure at times like these, especially when the pilot and the controller are acquainted. His vectors finally brought us face to face with a decision. The clouds began to lower and we were losing visibility quickly. All at once the cloud in front of us lit up and it showed a roll cloud all the way to the ground. From what I knew of roll clouds, I didn't want any part of one and this one could swallow us for sure. We turned away from the storms. The trip back through the first line entailed more of the original chaos. We returned to Dallas unscathed but I had a question on my mind: Why did the airborne radar show something different from the controller's unit?

A visit to my friend, Ben, at approach control helped explain the difference. He went into circular polarization and explained how it worked. It became evident that the ground radar was designed for better traffic following at the cost of weather detection. After all, an aircraft must be followed through areas of precipitation. If radar couldn't track a plane through rain and snow, then radar would be of dubious value in maintaining adequate separation between aircraft.

Perhaps we should mention the part that the transponder plays in tracking the plane through weather. As we discussed earlier, the circular polarization function serves to minimize weather returns. At the same time, the primary return of an aircraft not equipped with a transponder is also weakened. Hence, the invention of the transponder. A transponder, in essence, strengthens an incoming radar interrogation and sends the signal back. On occasion, a primary target (non-transponder) can be lost when travelling through rain or snow showers. Transponder equipped planes are rarely lost on radar due to the lack of signal return.

The most important thing we must learn about radar as pilots is that radar *cannot* detect turbulence. Ordinarily, the intensity of weather displayed is based on the precipitation density. More often than not, heavy turbulence is associated with the heaviest rainfall. This is because rain represents a downdraft situation. In recent years, new models for thunderstorms have been discovered and these have shown that there are narrow bands of turbulence or horizontal tornadoes, if you will, often between rain cells. This turbulence may materialize outside of rainfall areas. Thus, radar would be of no help in locating these violent air currents. It is this fact that makes it dangerous to fly through lines or clusters of thunderstorms by avoiding precipitation areas with radar. The choice sometimes comes down to completing the trip by the information at hand or cancelling. The safest way to fly thunderstorms in light aircraft is by remaining VFR below and out of clouds if at all possible, even if the plane is equipped with airborne radar.

ATC INFLIGHT WEATHER—AVOIDANCE ASSISTANCE

The IFR pilot is always on a flight plan and assigned route. It is obvious that any deviation at the whim of a pilot could throw a monkey wrench into the whole works. A change in altitude or flight level or any aberration off course requires a proper ATC clearance. However, if an immediate deviation is needed to avoid weather conditions that are hazardous to the safety of flight, the pilot may exercise his emergency authority.

Whenever a pilot needs a deviation from his assigned flight planned route he must ask ATC. The controller's job isn't as easy as just saying yes. The entire traffic picture must be surveyed in the affected area. Sometimes a deviation may have to be coordinated with other controllers if sector boundaries will be crossed. A great deal of flying time (or seemingly so to the pilot) may pass before the controller is ready with his reply.

Whenever we get ourselves into tight weather situations it is difficult to remember that the controller's primary responsibility is to provide safe separation between aircraft. Any additional service, such as weather avoidance assistance, can only be furnished to the extent that it does not derogate the primary function. Unfortunately, the separation workload becomes the greatest when weather disrupts the usual or normal flow of traffic. When one pilot is deviating, all the others follow suit and it seems everyone wants the same hole or altitude. Two other factors that influence the controller's ability to supply additional service are radar limitations and frequency congestion.

One other factor influences the amount of weather avoidance assistance that pilots get. That factor is how much responsibility the controller is willing to shoulder in guiding the aircraft through the least intense areas on his scope. Some controllers may have been burned by losing an aircraft in weather return areas. It is easy to see in such a case that the controller would be next to unwilling to aid the pilot. Then there are those that just shirk responsibility and let the pilot carry all the weight. This is not to say that the pilot is not responsible for everything, because he *is*, but the controller should be responsible to another human being who is in need of help.

I remember a controller at Chicago Center one night that merely replied "deviations of your choice approved. It all looks bad to me." As it turned out, we flew a terrible line of thunderstorms without ground radar assistance or airborne radar assistance and never hit a ripple. That night we were better off *without* him. It's just his attitude that torqued me off!

Knowing that some controllers may be reluctant to give weather avoidance advice can help us. At least if we surmise the controller is disinclined to help much, we can shift the conversation off center by asking probing questions. For example, we are flying in an area of broken thunderstorms. Out the window at two o'clock it looks to be a better route and sufficient room to safely maneuver between cells. The problem is that we don't know if the alley is a dead end or if it is indeed the safest passage. A question to the controller such as "Center 21 Echo, it looks a little better to us at two o'clock. Do you show any more cells back in that direction?" More often than not I've had even the most reluctant controllers come back with something similar to this: "21 Echo, there are two small areas of rain at your two o'clock position at 15 miles, but that does look like the best way to go." The probing question has gotten some useful information and the controller doesn't feel like his job is on the line if the pilot ventures off in that direction.

A pilot should remember that even when controllers furnish vectors for weather avoidance, he implies all headings as *suggestions*. Air traffic radar has limitations as we have already discussed. Therefore, if you get a bad ride, don't blame the controller. On the other hand, those reluctant, unwilling—to—help controllers ought to have their chair jacked up and down every once and a while to remind them that all is not so serene as the control room.

Earlier in my career, flying a regular freight run from Minneapolis to Chicago to Pittsburgh every night, weather avoidance was a regular thing. On a trip that long there were usually thunderstorms somewhere along the route. Having flown all over the U.S., I have noticed that clearance to deviate is longer in coming the further east one is travelling. This is probably due to the heavy influx of traffic to the northeast where the overall traffic picture includes hundreds of planes at a time. Just the same we had a standard line that "…. they have to run the clearance through the White House and the President must be in the bathroom." Honestly, I've seen clearances to deviate so slow in coming that we almost had to exercise our emergency authority.

It is extremely important therefore that any request for deviation or radar vector be forwarded to ATC as far in advance as possible. Simply put, if you see lightning or dark clouds ahead and center has you at 10,000 feet, the request for lower or higher should be made immediately. Delay in submitting a request may delay or even preclude ATC approval. That means one might be forced into a dangerous position where life or death decisions are imminent.

Whenever possible, the following information should be provided to ATC when requesting a clearance to get out of the messy weather. The proposed point where the detour will commence, if it is not from the present position, is the logical place to begin. Then, if one knows the direction and distance to deviate, forward that to the controller. Obviously, the original route will be resumed at some point unless a totally new clearance is desired. It is best to give the controller your best idea as to where you will rejoin the original flight planned route. The controller will always appreciate the reason you want to deviate and a report on the ride. Also, if an aircraft is equipped with functioning weather radar, deviations may be more readily approved, so tell them *that*, too. If any further deviations are needed after leaving the planned route, don't be afraid to ask for deviations from the deviation. Often, flying areas of showers require a great deal of snaking around.

Since we discussed earlier some radio techniques involving clarity and brevity, let's put our new knowledge into action. Here is the way a competent IFR pilot would ask for a deviation off course:

"Center, 21 Echo, we are painting a cell at 12 o'clock and would like to turn left 15 degrees to pass it to the south. We should be able to rejoin Victor 189 in about 20 miles."

"Roger 21 Echo, deviation approved; maintain present altitude."

In our transmission, though it wasn't terribly short, we covered all questions in the controller's mind. The guidelines that we set forth to request a deviation for weather have been followed. All the controller needs to do is to check his scope for conflicting traffic at your altitude. Chances are that he is painting the area of weather also and can see clearly the route we intend to fly.

After we have flown the deviation off course we have a responsibility to our brothers. There may be planes only a few miles behind us or coming down the airway from the other side that may need to deviate as well. The thing to do is make a pilot report to the controller:

"Center, 21 Echo, the ride was fairly good. We only had light rain and remained VFR. There was some moderate chop at 23 DME off the Vortac."

I always feel good when, after making a report such as this, the controller comes back with a response like this: "21 Echo, roger, 53 Bravo did you copy that?" It is evident that some other aircraft is in the same area and needed that information. The only drawback sometimes is that someone needs to be the scout. That means flying unexplored weather territory at times. The challenge and the satisfaction of success often balance each other and helping someone else just adds to the feeling.

GETTING ALONG WITH ATC

The climate in recent years has often grown to a battle for power between pilots and controllers. This comes from the feeling that controllers feel they can best make decisions as to where planes should go or not go. It is the feeling of the fraternity of pilots that decisions affecting the operation of an aircraft *cannot* be made from the ground. After all, who is closer to the situation, the controller miles away in a darkened room (Fig. 3-4), or the pilot in

Fig. 3-4. The controllers have their guidelines and problems, too. As a result, we should give them our consideration during peak periods. This photo was shot in very dark conditions; thus some of the controllers are blurred due to movement.

the cockpit? To us pilots, the choice is clear. The problem is that ATC has us over a barrel quite often. Because of this fact, it becomes necessary for us to learn how to compromise with ATC. Many times what we would *like* in a clearance and what we will *get* are quite different. Sometimes the proper question will bend a rigid situation into a more flexible one.

There are times when it is imperative to file instruments due to weather enroute or at the destination. The departure point, however, may be perfectly good VFR. In metropolitan areas, where there is heavy traffic, possibly even a TCA with arriving and departing jets, ATC may hold the aircraft at what seems to be an unnecessarily low altitude. Often in VFR weather an altitude of three or four thousand feet may be quite bumpy. Already suspecting this, a pilot usually files for a much higher altitude. The problem comes when we ask for a climb to escape the turbulence. The controller replies that due to inbound traffic he must hold you low for at least another ten minutes. In a condition that is uncomfortable to passengers, it is up to the pilot to find a way out of the bumps. A possible solution is to compromise and ask for a VFR climb. This implies that the pilot is willing to accept fully the "see and avoid" concept of traffic control. There should be no problem with this if the weather is good VFR such as scattered clouds and ten miles visibility. The controller may accept this as a workable solution, but issue a VFR-on-top clearance. Go ahead and accept the clearance. Once you are through the critical altitudes ask to resume the normal IFR posture. In order not to make a nuisance of myself, I generally wait for a frequency change to the next sector. Then upon establishing radio communication with the next controller, request a change from a VFR-on-top altitude to an IFR altitude.

Another situation that frequently occurs is a need for another altitude. Turbulence, icing, or thunderstorms are common reasons to request a change in flight level or altitude. An item that many of us forget is that we can request any altitude when we are IFR. In other words, regardless of the direction of flight, we may request 5, 6, or 7 thousand, for instance. It is customary for us to file odd-thousands of feet east bound and even thousands west bound. The thing to remember is that not all altitudes are being utilized in our areas; at least rarely is this the case. A request for a higher or lower altitude will usually follow suit if it is granted. If the altitude that we are flying is odd then the altitude granted will be odd also.

We were flying level at 4,000 feet when we began to pick up traces of ice. The winds aloft forecast suggested a temperature of +2 degrees Celsius at 6,000 feet. That meant warmer air should be just above. We asked for 6,000 feet and got it. The only problem was that it still was right at freezing and we were still in the clouds. 8,000 feet would give us more headwind so we asked for a compromise. "Any chance for 7,000?", we querried. The immediate reply was climb and maintain 7,000 feet. Fortunately, no one else was at 7,000 feet in the area and as it turned out it was the best altitude to be flying that day.

Situations when flying IFR cannot always be changed. For example, flying into the Dallas-Fort Worth Regional Airport during cloudy conditions means that metering will be in effect. What this means is that *exact* spacing and speed restrictions are imposed by the controllers. Under such circumstances, there is little chance for getting anything but a published arrival route.

During hours just before light and around midnight, the traffic is light. Regardless if conditions are IFR or not a pilot can usually ask for a "direct" clearance to shorten the flight and receive it. There is generally not enough traffic to restrict a flight to the round-about flight plans that we ordinarily have to fly. The rule should be to always ask for direct. It saves fuel and precious time of which there never seem to be enough. The exception to the rule is whenever "metering" is in force.

A pilot who is not familiar with metering procedures can usually identify them by listening to the controller. After checking in with approach control, listen for his chatter with the airlines. If he is handing out speed restriction such as "cross Farina at 11,000 at 270 knots," then they are metering. If the controller states something like "you may delete the speed . . . " then metering may not be in effect. In this case, a request for "direct" may be granted. The best advice is to use discretion and good sense. The reason I say this is that a memo from DFW approach control recently came down to our airline proclaiming a 41% increase in flights through their area in the first nine months of 1979. In the memo they request that all airlines not ask for direct clearances, and stated if at all possible the controller would issue them on his own initiative if traffic permitted. Of course, a lightplane pilot flying into a secondary airport at low altitudes might have better luck.

One of the things I hated when I was flying for a charter operation was calling for clearance prior to taxi and receiving something totally different than what I filed. There are two reasons this is a bad deal. One, the clearance is difficult to copy because it usually is very long, containing names of Vortacs, and intersections that are not familiar. Two, the pilot usually misses most of it because it creates confusion in his mind as to where the heck is that intersection.

An item that is most always covered adequately in instrument rating ground schools is that of preferred routes. The trouble is that very often, even during training flights, these preferred routes are not filed. A preferred IFR route is a route that is listed or described in a publication and designed to smooth the flow of air traffic in, out and through busy areas. Often, outbound traffic will be cleared on a Victor airway such as V77E. The inbound traffic from the same general direction will be delivered via V77.

Filing preferred routes will eliminate the confusing clearance problem we alluded to earlier. As matter of fact the clearance one has to copy becomes a joke. The controller will just say "cleared as filed . . .,"and that is easy to write when using clearance shorthand. Besides the ease of copying the clearance, the confusion factor is eliminated. The pilot already has in his mind the route he is expecting to fly. Many times the smooth reception of an expected clearance sets the stage for a smooth flight. Conversely, a clearance that is confusing may set the stage for confusion during the ensuing flight in any of several areas.

Flying instruments takes a great deal of mental agility. An instrument flight takes mental preparation similar to that an athlete utilizes to prepare for a big game, not to mention the physical preparation of flight plan. Those preferred routes we were talking about can be found in your Jeppesen book or a current Airman's Information Manual. After a pilot has flown a route a couple of times the flight plan becomes familiar. At least the clearance one receives if it is other than "as filed" can be memorized and filed that way on later flights.

Speaking of the physical preparation of flight plans, few things can be done to make the flight go smoother. Passenger comfort should always be foremost in a pilot's mind. One of the things that ATC does invariably on every flight is leave the aircraft high until near the initial approach fix. Believe it or not, the point at which the descent should begin can be planned during the initial flight planning. Rules of thumb such as 180 knots equals 3 miles per minute can be used to roughly estimate the point at which the descent should be intiated.

Just to refresh the memory, let's cover such a let-down exercise. Let's pretend that our flight planned altitude toward the end of the flight is six thousand feet. The destination is good enough for visual approaches and field elevation is approximately 1,000 feet. In other words, we will have to lose 5,000 feet before we land. In smoother descent, meaning one that is not stepped down 1,000 feet at a time, we should plan to lose the standard 500 feet per minute. It will take 10 minutes to lose that 5,000 feet at 500 feet per minute. At 180 knots the aircraft will travel 30 miles in that 10 minutes. Therefore, the descent should be started 30 miles out from the destination.

In theory, this practice works out fine. It will always work if we are flying VFR free from radar separation such as Stage 3 services. When we are IFR, though, ATC does not usually allow a smooth gradual descent. The controller, being bound by certain rules of operation ordinarily must stair-step the airplane from altitude to altitude. In this case the plane can chew up far *more* than the 30 miles we just discussed. The end result is rapid altitude changes as the aircraft quickly approaches the airfield and that mounts up to ear and sinus discomfort for passengers. Particularly when infants are on board it becomes necessary to avoid this type of operation if at all possible. Infants are most sensitive to pressure changes because they don't understand nor do they know how to cope with the pain. Let's face it, who needs a screaming baby during an instrument approach to minimums?

What all this leads up to is the fact that we must request our descents ahead of time. A good fudge factor is 25%. Increase the necessary distance to descend by 25% and mark that on the enroute chart during flight planning. Whenever we cross that point during the flight that should be the time we initiate a call to ATC and request a lower altitude. If the request is granted promptly, just decrease the rate of descent. That makes the passengers' ride that much more comfortable.

Occasionally, the converse of this situation occurs and ATC will ask us to descend ahead of time. A good idea in a case of this nature is to ask if the descent is at pilot's discretion. Perhaps the altitudes below hold ice, and staying high until the last minute is safer (Fig. 3-5). If this is explained to the controller, many times your request will be honored. Often, safety becomes the predominant consideration over passenger comfort. Pilot's discretion type of clearances are a handy item at times.

There are times when ATC cannot issure a "PD" clearance. At those times, however, a controller may let us stay at the desired altitude a little longer. Sometimes, the length of time that we are allowed to stay high may not be what is necessary in our minds, but like so many things is life it is a compromise. Sharing the airspace with others requires that sometimes we must give in for their safety. After all, their safety is important too.

Fig. 3-5. Sometimes the altitudes below hold ice. It is probably a good idea to ask for a descent at pilot's discretion and stay high.

Flying IFR to one's best advantage takes practice and an open ear. One of the best ways to learn IFR practices is to invest in an aircraft band radio. The new digital scanners are real handy for finding the active frequencies in the area. Listening to the chatter, a newly rated instrument pilot can pick out the good and bad habits rather quickly. Sitting at home in the easy chair is a much better learning environment than the cockpit. At least, until a pilot becomes comfortable in the IFR environment, keeping the plane upright and the needles centered necessarily becomes the center of concentration.

Hopefully, we have covered most of the items that go untaught in instrument curricula. Perhaps at this time some of the ideas seem vague. However, a little experience will *now* go a long way. Each pilot who has read this chapter will readily identify with these situations as they crop up. It may not be a conscious transfer of information to the practical application. Rather, it will seem like the natural thing to do—and that's just what we have been shooting for.

Chapter 4
The Transition
Problem

Ragged ceilings, loosely strung across the airport, have too often claimed the souls of pilots and their friends at the outset of their journey. Conspicuous as they are, they have befuddled the minds of pilots who were most adequately prepared for the IFR jaunt from the mythical point A. They were prepared, that is, with the exception of the mental agility required in preparation for the takeoff. In a situation where instrument conditions will begin at 200 feet (Fig. 4-1), the transition often is not smooth but rather abrupt. The rough edges of clouds may indicate turbulence and turbulence may contribute to the rapid onset of vertigo. That is exactly what happened to Piper Arrow 35V on takeoff on an early spring flight.

Arrow 35 V was cleared into position to hold. The takeoff roll began as soon as the tower released him for IFR. The pilot was a male in his early 30s with about 250 total hours and 60 hours of instrument flight of which only 20 was actual; a good pilot by many standards. The pilot had checked weather and planned quite well for the flight ahead. As the Arrow disappeared in the clouds the gear was just being retracted. Neighbors to the airport on the departure end of the runway reported hearing the plane's engine racing, then fading, as if the plane was on a roller coaster track and then .... silence.

The accident investigation reconstructed this scene in the plane's cockpit. As the pilot pulled to a stop on the active runway, he reached down and set his directional gyro and activated the transponder. The pilot applied takeoff power and the aircraft lifted off normally.

The weather that morning was an indefinite 200 feet and one mile in light rain and fog. The wind was gusting to 15 knots which would indicate at least light turbulence could be expected after takeoff. As the pilot of Arrow 35V reached the 200-foot ceiling, he reached down for the gear actuator switch. Almost simultaneously, the Arrow penetrated the belly of the overcast. The combination of light turbulence and the pilot's momentary inattention to a non-control item (gear retraction) was enough to induce vertigo. The resulting confusion and the inability of the relatively inexperienced pilot in actual instrument conditions to recover his instrument scan was cited as the cause of this accident.

As with so many general aviation accidents, the underlying or basic reason was a lack of experience. Unfortunately, experience must be gained at some risk. In this particular case the accident could have been avoided by the pilot doing a few things. When a pilot's experience factor is low for a particular operation, such as a low ceiling and visibility takeoff, then extra caution should be taken to offset the odds.

The first thing a pilot should do is a cockpit instrument check. This instrument check should be done during the taxi to the runway. Of course, we may have other checklists to be run during this time as well, yet neglecting the instrument check may prove expensive if not terrifying.

In this cockpit check we should pay *strict* attention to the flight instruments. The engine instruments will be checked according to our before takeoff check or run-up. Probably the first instrument we should check is the altimeter. At tower controlled airports, the correct altimeter setting will be passed on to us via the Automatic Terminal Information Service (ATIS) or by the ground controller as we request permission to taxi. Setting the altimeter to the proper barometric setting should reflect the field elevation. That is what we are looking for. The altimeter is unusable for IFR if the indicated altitude is plus or minus 75 feet from field elevation. Most altimeters will reveal some error, even those with bellows compensators such as encoding altimeters. Encoding altimeters are generally more accurate due to the fact that they have a compensator which allows the bellows to expand more homogenously through all altitudes.

Vertical speed indicators occasionally get out of kilter. On a cockpit check we are checking to make sure the needle is indicating a zero rate of climb or descent. If the instrument is showing something other than zero, two things can be done. One, the pilot

Fig. 4-1. This photo was shot when the weather was 200 and a ½. A takeoff in this type of weather takes a great deal of forethought and some practice. It is also very useful to have some experience at this sort of situation.

can make a mental note and correct throughout the flight for it. For example, if the VSI shows a 100 feet per minute climb, that 100 feet must be subtracted to all climbs to obtain the correct value. Conversely, most descents should be about 500 feet per minute and the 100 feet per minute error must be added to all descents for the proper value.

The second thing that can be done is to adjust the instrument itself. The legality of a pilot being able to adjust the instrument without being a FAA licensed aircraft mechanic lies in one of those gray areas in the regulations. This much can be said: it *is* done commonly by many and it never has been cited as a cause for an accident.

The instrument can be re-zeroed by adjusting the set screw on the lower left-hand corner with a screwdriver. This should be done while the aircraft is on the ground and preferably not faced into the wind during gusty conditions. Gusty winds can sometimes cause erroneous readings. Let's face it, if the airplane is on the ground there should be no question that the rate of change should be zero. That's why setting the VSI in the air may do more harm than good.

The other instruments should be checked during turns while taxiing. The directional gyro, if operating properly, will show a decrease in the heading numbers if turning left, and will increase in a turn to the right. Don't just glance at the DG to see if it is turning. A failed DG may tumble back and forth and there is no telling which way it will be going.

Usually, the only electric instrument is the turn and bank indicator. In partial panel situations, the turn and bank or turn coordinator can be a life saver. Having flown with both turn and bank and turn coordinators, there seems to be no major advantage to either one. However, I do recall reading about an accident involving main gyro failure in an airliner cockpit. The crew went to the turn coordinator and confused it with the horizon indicator. In left turn the coordinator's left wing goes down. If you think about that, it is just *opposite* from the horizon indicator. Thus, the crew became confused and vertigo set in and ruined the trip for everyone. With either instrument, the idea is to check that it is functioning at all. The failed T & B's I have seen don't move at all if they have failed for some reason. Some aircraft have circuit breakers for the T & B, so don't taxi back in if you find the instrument inoperative until you check those breakers!

The attitude gyro should be checked during a turn. As everyone knows, the horizon indicator does *not* bank in a turn on the ground. That is, unless it is broken . This instrument is vacuum powered, ordinarily. The proper response would be to check the vacuum gauge to ascertain whether it has failed since engine start. Most horizon indicators will show a small bank during a turn. Any bank more than 5 degrees should be considered unacceptable for instrument flight.

The only other flight instrument left in the cluster is the airspeed indicator. Unfortunately, there is no way to check if it is working. However, in anticipation of flight into clouds during even cool conditions, the pitot heat should be flipped on to ensure the instrument doesn't fail during climb out.

Another thing the pilot of 35V could have done was to clean the airplane up before punching into the clouds. Although most instructors would teach a student of a complex airplane not to retract the gear before the end of the runway or until a positive rate of climb is established, a low ceiling must necessarily change that. As soon as one is sure the airplane is not going to settle back on its gear the switch should be moved to the "up" position. At all costs the clean up process should be done before entering the clouds or well after the instrument scan has been established. Ordinarily, a good procedure is to grab the gear handle first and leave the flaps until after entering the overcast. Be careful not to exceed flap speed. But this is good, in a way, because it establishes a cross check early in the duties of scanning.

Obviously, the most important liability is establishing an instrument scan early. In fact, the scan should be begun *before* entering the clouds. The ability to do this can be learned in a short time. This ability comes from practicing zero-zero takeoffs. The FAA believes this develops the necessary scan during takeoff roll that can and will be continued into the flight. Clearly, it will make the transition from VFR conditions to instrument meteorological conditions (IMC) simpler. Had the pilot of 35V had this training the flight might have proceeded without incident. What goes into a good zero-zero takeoff? Let's take a look.

ZERO-ZERO TAKEOFF

No matter how remote one may consider the chance of making an IFR departure under totally zero conditions, the knowledge and ability to do so carries well into one's IFR capabilities and strengthens the experience level. If you are career oriented, then a blind departure may become a reality some day. Departures in one-quarter mile visibility are *regular* occurences at my airline.

Proficiency at this maneuver builds confidence at all levels of IFR flying and as we have already stated, a rapid transition from visual to instrument flight conditions can result in serious disorientation and control problems.

Instrument takeoff techniques vary between types of aircraft but the basic method described below will work in any plane. The most important facet of this maneuver is runway alignment. Pull out to the centerline and roll a short distance to ensure the aircraft is tracking down the stripes. Failure to do this may result in the plane being off just a few degrees. That could be enough to wipe out a taxi light or two prior to lift off. Once the plane is in position, lock the tailwheel if it is so equipped and hold the brakes firmly to avoid creeping while preparing for the takeoff.

Next, set the heading indicator or DG with the nose index on the 5 degree mark nearest the published runway heading. This will enable us to detect the slightest change in direction during the takeoff roll. The published runway heading we refer to is that in the approach plates. For example, runway 35 may have a heading of 352 degrees. Set the DG on 350 even. After setting the heading indicator be sure it is uncaged. There's nothing more frightening to tower controllers than a plane speedily ambling in their direction. Another good idea is to set the heading bug if your instrument is so equipped. If using an HSI, set the heading bug, but don't change the VOR needle to other than the course expected after takeoff. The reason for this is that it may cause unneeded distraction after takeoff when most attention should be given to the scan.

After setting the heading indicator and receiving clearance from the tower (assuming there is one), advance the throttle to an RPM that provides partial rudder control. Release the brakes, and advance the power smoothly. As you release the brakes, expect a left turn from torque and P-factor. Maintain a constant heading (the one you set) by rudder control. In multi-engine, differential power can be used to some extent to maintain directional control. One thing we don't want to do is to use brakes for directional control. Brakes will cause overcontrol and extend the takeoff roll. Remember, any deviation in heading must be corrected *instantly*. That makes the heading indicator the primary reference during takeoff.

As the aircraft accelerates, begin cross-checking the DG and the airspeed indicator rapidly. As flying speed nears, apply elevator control smoothly and monitor the attitude indicator for the desired takeoff attitude. This should be approximately a 2-bar-width climb indication for most light aircraft. In larger planes, the nose attitude may range from seven to fifteen degrees.

As the takeoff continues, the scan should also continue. It is important not to pull the airplane off, but let it fly off. In that way we can be sure the plane will establish a positive rate of climb on its own. When the aircraft becomes airborne, maintain pitch and bank control by reference to the attitude indicator and begin coordinated corrections rather than using just rudder.

At this point we begin bringing all the other instruments into the scan. Check the altimeter and vertical speed indicator for a positive rate of climb. Once you have satisfied yourself by experience that the plane is climbing, raise the gear and flaps. At this point we should be about 100 feet in the air and scanning perfectly well. Yet, under most departure conditions we would not be in the clouds.

Gear and flap retraction usually create pitch changes. Overcontrolling is likely unless we note the attitude changes and trim off the control pressures quickly. Once the climb has been stabilized to some extent, we can smoothly accelerate to a predetermined climb speed. At climb speed, reduce the power unless full power is recommended; then trim.

Throughout this exercise, cross-check and interpretation

must be quick and the control positive and smooth. Be sure to anticipate control pressure changes as gear and flaps are raised and during power reduction. Rapid scanning is the key to success in this exercise.

Among the common errors during zero-zero takeoffs is the failure to perform an adequate cockpit check *before* the takeoff. Incredible as it sounds, students have attempted instrument takeoffs with gyros caged, airspeed indicators inoperative (pitot tube obstructed), controls locked and other tomfoolery. Needless to say, precious few have mastered the instrument takeoff under these handicaps.

Proper alignment with the runway seems to be one of the biggest problems. Many times, improper alignment is the result of differential brake application. Sometimes the aircraft is allowed to creep after alignment. Occasionally this problem will result from the tailwheel being locked prematurely or the nosewheel cocked. One thing for sure: any of these oversights will start the plane in an odd direction. What's worse is when the plane is canted slightly to one side or another and the DG is set to the runway heading. In this case, any effort to keep the heading precise after the roll has begun will result in a continuance in the odd direction.

An abrupt application of power creates directional control problems. Too often, the student will jam the power in and the nose will swing the the left. The rest of the takeoff is then complicated by trying to recover from this one error.

Over-controlling on the rudder pedals is a common mistake. The root of this particular problem however, can be traced to the pilot's instrument scan. Late recognition of heading changes or misinterpretation of the heading indicator causes a swerving until lift-off. Many pilots fail to realize the effectiveness of the rudder in making changes. More than likely, an increased rate of scan will take care of all these problems.

One of the most dangerous mistakes is attempting to fly the airplane by "seat-of-the-pants" sensations after becoming airborne. It is essential that the proper attitude is maintained by reference to the attitude indicator. The pitch changes that come with gear and flap retraction can cause motion sensations that cannot be coped with in any other way but a good instrument scan.

Fixation on one instrument or another is an error. During trim changes a pilot is likely to watch only one instrument, such as the airspeed indicator. While doing this the wing may dip and the heading begins to wander. The problems may compound from there. An adequate cross-check or scan takes care of this problem.

A few practice instrument takeoffs with an appropriate safety pilot can build all the confidence an IFR pilot needs for handling low ceiling and visibility takeoffs in actuality. Besides the confidence, the level of skill and proficiency of the pilot is elevated, enabling him to tackle the job at hand. Undoubtedly, the toughest parts of an IFR flight are the transitions from VFR to IFR and back again. These transitions may happen several times during a flight, not just at the beginning or the end.

The flight through cloud tops or rising and falling tops entails a transition of sorts (Fig. 4-2). The one thing that new instrument pilots must guard against is flying by visual cues once breaking out on top. Often the cloud decks are tilted, possibly several degrees. Aligning the wings or your visual reference cue to a tilting cloud deck will cause some sort of problem, if not vertigo. If a pilot is conned into believing that clouds layers are perfectly horizontal and then engages when they are not, the instrument references will appear to be unreliable.

If a pilot begins believing that instrument references are unreliable, the safe outcome of the flight may then be in question. A pilot then might assume that during the descent the instruments may need to be compensated for. The result would be a constant turning in one direction and eventually complete disorientation.

The problem of not believing the instruments is not likely to happen to the veteran IFR pilot. The problem that is encountered more often is the momentary feelings of vertigo as the plane bursts through the glaring white tops of cumulus. The airplane actually penetrates a cloud top with such rapidity that no time is available for transition to instrument references. Moreover, the tops of cumulus clouds usually contain wind demons of some sort. A sudden updraft at the moment all outside reference is stolen from us only complicates the task of remaining upright.

To begin with, most aircraft are inherently stable, especially after the plane is trimmed for level flight. One of the things an instrument pilot learns is that flying instruments is *not* a physical thing. Rather, the pilot is herding the plane down a path, only correcting as it begins to stray. It takes finesse. Once a pilot can consciously realize that fact, remaining upright becomes much easier even under partial panel conditions. Applying this to punching the bumpy tops of cumulus, we simply monitor the airplane in its effort to return to a stable trimmed condition.

Fig. 4-2. Punching through cloud tops requires a transition of sorts.

The other things we can do before probing cloud uppers is prepare ahead of time. We can see the tufts of cloud rushing at us. We should transition to instrument references prior to entrance into the cloud. Usually, the air is smoother outside the cloud than it will be inside, and it is best to begin the transition early. Also, once inside the cloud's upper parts the turbulence may effect our inner ear to a great enough extent that transition to instrument references becomes a forced exercise of mind over matter. Making the transition early simplifies matters. Throughout an IFR flight, we may have to make these inflight adjustments several times.

THE HOME STRETCH

He tightened the strap under his chin and tucked his scarf in his jacket. Sliding the throttle back, he gently eased the stick to its most aft position. As the plane shuddered in rebellion to that treatment, he put his foot into the rudder. The wind began to batter his face again. Vaguely, images began to spin in front of him. The rudder was neutralized and the back pressure released. The old yellow biplane began to fly again, soaring out of the overcast like an enraged eagle. Spotting the airfield in the distance, he flew toward home. The wheels slithered through the grass still wet from a morning shower. The tail swung into place in front of the hangar as the mail pilot's day ended.

They tell me that's the way it was in the earliest days of "blind" flying. The pilot stayed upright using a turn and bank and followed a compass across the country. When he got to the destination he simply spun down through the clouds and recovered when he achieved visual conditions. I hope none of them ever tried that when it was 200 and a half! As it was, there was little or no transition from inside the cockpit to references outside the cockpit. In actuality, the pilot had his head up and looking for visual references the entire time after the spin had begun. I'm sure it didn't take very long for pilots (or anyone with any sense at all) to discover how unsatisfactory *this* procedure was.

As radio became developed, the first simple units found their way into the cockpit. Soon radio navigation appeared to be the wave of the future. Indeed it was. The first instrument approaches using radio navigation were invented. Soon after, it became evident that special lighting was needed to find the runway in low visibility conditions. Being able to descend below the clouds under control wasn't enough. As every instrument pilot knows, the runway or the runway environment must be in sight. After some simple lighting systems came into operation a new problem cropped up. The runways could be found more easily, but in sloppy weather, depth perception became a problem. There are several reasons why depth perception suffers during marginal weather. But the one that gets most of us modern day pilots is the transition from IFR to VFR conditions: the changing of the focal point of our vision from only a couple feet (the flight instruments) to infinity.

The transition from "blind" conditions to visual conditions has been enhanced by modern approach lighting systems and a marvelous invention called VASI. The Visual Approach Slope Indicator is designed to give the same information that the glide slope indicator is designed to give; the same information that the glide slope unit of an ILS gives electronically, only in visual cues. The VASI streams out a light path of 2.5 to 4 degrees from the horizontal throughout the approach zone. Course guidance is obtained by aligning the aircraft with the approach and runway lights.

The standard VASI unit consists of a 12-light source arranged in bars. The upwind bars are usually placed at 600 feet from the runway threshold. The downwind bars are about 1300 feet from the threshold. If the pilot guides his plane down the visual glide slope the touchdown point will be halfway in between. Ordinarily, in good flying weather, the VASI can be used with accuracy from about the middle marker. At night we can use them from quite a ways out and that is *highly* recommended for straight-in approaches.

The flying chores are made a great deal easier by a VASI. It doesn't make any difference whether one is shooting an ILS, precision approach or a non-precision approach. Coming down the tube through the murk can be an anxious time. Many a sigh of relief has been breathed after seeing the approach lights and a VASI to finish the trek to the ground.

As we were discussing the transition from blind to a sighted approach, we should cover a couple of pointers. Your instrument instructor probably covered this one long ago, but it still holds true. *Don't* look up until the missed approach point (MAP) or DH has been reached! But, like any other good rule, there are exceptions. The good Lord blessed us with peripheral vision and we should use it. I don't know of anybody with at least Class III medical vision who cannot see the ground start moving under the plane after breaking out of the clouds. On an ILS it might be a good idea to take a peek for the runway, if our peripheral vision says we are below the junk. Before looking, however, pay attention enough to your peripheral vision to notice if wisps of clouds are going by. It could be that we can see down, but due to a ragged ceiling may not be able to see forward. The result would be that necessary concentration is removed from the flight instruments and perhaps the accuracy of the approach would suffer.

Non-precision approaches are a little different ball game. Minimum Descent Altitudes are not correlated with the missed approach point. One could arrive at the missed approach time and the MDA simultaneously, but that isn't a good practice either. Because we usually descend to the MDA well before time to execute the miss, it may be a good idea to peek early in an effort to adjust to visual references while at a high enough altitude for mistakes. If the runway we are approaching is equipped with VASI, we may be able to intercept the glide slope instead of flying through it. As you know, flying through the visual approach slope would require a much higher rate of descent to re-intercept it. This brings in two other problems. Too high a rate of descent for passenger comfort, and a high rate of sink that must be arrested at some point. Therefore, on non-precision approaches, use the peripheral vision technique to predetermine if the aircraft is indeed at or below the cloud bases.

To reiterate, if there is any doubt about being below the clouds prior to the MAP or the DH then keep your head down and eyes glued to those flight instruments. Once at the MAP or DH, the decision has to be made to land or go around. If a pilot is by himself,

Fig. 4-3. This an ILS runway without VASI. In low visibility conditions the best bet is to ride the glideslope down to the threshold.

the only thing to do is look up. Take a good two or three seconds to scan the windshield and the two side windows. Based on what one sees then execute the miss or land.

Another thing that can be done is to use the aid of a pilot friend. We don't always have a pilot with us to help. However, a pilot can spot the runway for us if it comes into view prior to the MAP. If it isn't in view at the MAP, then both parties should take one long hard look. It is advised not to use a non-pilot for spotting the runway. They are not used to the appearance of airports in general from the air and may call a highway a runway. In your effort to double check them, you may lose the approach altogether.

A note of interest is the way the airlines do it. There are two methods. The non-flying pilot usually monitors the altimeter during the approach and looks outside for the runway and its environment. When it is in sight the non-flier calls it in sight. The pilot flying the aircraft now alternates between the flight instruments that are providing navigation (and usually glide slope information), and visual reference with the runway. The transition is therefore carried through in steps, so to speak.

The other method in use for many years by British Airways and recently finding favor with some U.S. airlines is the visual pilot taking control of the airplane and performing the landing. That's right: the pilot *not* flying the instrument approach takes over and makes the landing. At this time, it is my understanding that

Eastern Airlines is using this method and that American Airlines is doing some experimenting with it. If the professionals find the transition from cockpit references to outside references a bit difficult, then low time instrument pilots should be wary.

One of the things a good instrument pilot can do to aid the transition is to alternate between the ILS instruments and the runway. Many ILS runways do not have VASI, although the majority do (Fig. 4-3). Approaches at night in low visibility conditions (Fig. 4-4) are the greatest temptation for a pilot to descend, even *dive at*, the runway. Many accident reports describe how the pilot, after reporting "runway in sight," landed short of that runway. Of course, this goes back to our depth perception

Fig. 4-4. Transitions at night are a different ball game. There is no VASI on this runway. The strobe lights can add to the difficulty in foggy conditions.

problem. Where VASI is not present we must rely on our wits. The wise thing to do is follow the glide slope down to the runway. During non-precision approaches, the best technique is to imagine the landing point at the end of the first third of runway. Aim for that point.

DOING IT BACKWARDS

The most difficult and precarious approach I've ever had the chance to witness was in fog. The approach was to a runway that was ILS equipped. Sitting in the jump seat, I had a bird's eye view of the entire spectacle. The situation was an odd one. The visibility was being reported as a half mile and the ceiling as indefinite 100 feet. From our vantage point approaching the airport, it became evident the weather looked different from ground than from the air. The truth was, there *was* no ceiling! Stars adorned the night, surrounding the plane. The fog was only a thin layer in much the same manner that silt covers the bottom of a beautiful lake.

The fog reached from what seemed about 200 feet down to the ground. As we flew over, the lights on the ground were perfectly visible. They seemed to just invite us home. Looking far ahead, toward the airport, it was like a battle. The airport beacon swept through the fog like a laser. The sequenced flashers exploded in the fog like depth charges detonating beneath a glassy sea.

As we started down the glide path, it became clear that we wouldn't reach the misty envelope until the decision height. What a decision! Finally we descended to decision altitude. The lights were all there, lighting the fog up like the Las Vegas strip. Well, the rules say if you have the runway environment in sight it is legal to land. Sure enough, we were legal all right, but this was instrument flying in reverse. Aren't the visibility conditions supposed to improve at the DH on an approach in minumum weather? Not tonight. They got *worse*. Certainly, a situation where the pilot must adapt quickly if safety is to be assured.

Thinking about that night it becomes apparent there is precious little in any pilot's training or experience to make that task easier. On a runway without VASI such as this one, the only technique had to be one of rapid alternating between the dismal, mist, almost mirage-like visual references and the flight instruments on the panel. The pilot flying the approach that evening was highly experienced and up to handling the difficulties. Surely, the best aid he had was to follow the glide slope down until the strobes were behind him. Then upon reaching an altitude of near 50 feet, he relied upon the runway lights for course guidance and depth perception. Possibly he monitored the VSI for a shallow rate of descent. There is no doubt the problems posed by that approach can be handled adequately, but there is no time to fixate on any one instrument or visual cue. To do that would only be an invitation to scrape the airplane against something unyielding.

Probably, experience had everything to do with the success of that approach. Yet, it would be unusual if a pilot had ever seen that same situation before. It probably only happens once in every 10,000 hours of flying. Two or three times might be all a pilot would experience it in a career. Unquestionably, the first time around with it *is* an *experience*!

It seems that the transition from VFR to IFR or the converse requires skill. It is an acquired skill. Newly rated instrument pilots must go through that learning experience. Hopefully, we have uncovered a few of the secrets in doing it properly. Reading this chapter is in no way a substitute for experience. However, raising one's consciousness may reduce the risk in the learning process. The pilot that can relax in his armchair and give the subject a few moments thought may stack the cards in his favor. The next time it is your turn to deal with IFR transitions, you'll know what will turn up.

Chapter 5
Inflight Decisions

For better or worse—that's what is on the line every time the flight plan is altered. The flight plan? That's right. Any change in altitude, course direction or landing airport is a deviation from flight plan. Before the flight plan *is* altered a pilot must make a decision to do so. At times, these very decisions may mean life or death, not just smoother air or less ice.

The basis for decisions is experience and learning. There are two ways to learn without doing: lecture or reading, as you are doing now. Experience, on the other hand, comes by risking something. Most times one doesn't actually risk his neck to learn. Flying, ordinarily is not that dramatic. Sometimes, though, one may risk his reputation as a "smooth" pilot in a quest for the best route around rain showers. That's all right though; many times the anxiety of the challenge produces an immense feeling of accomplishment. Unfortunately, non-flying passengers rarely appreciate the significance of what has just been done. But that's flying, and part of what each pilot must suffer in his pursuit of experience.

When one makes the decision to get that instrument ticket, he should also decide that he will *use* it. The pilot who gets the rating, then *doesn't* use it to advantage is throwing money away. If a pilot flies in conjunction with business, the necessity is there. Yet, many businessmen/pilots fail to attack a flying situation in the same professional manner that they would a business deal. Therein lies a big secret. A pilot must be able to separate his or her other daily activities from flying. When one takes the left seat he or she becomes a *pilot*. That's all, just a pilot.

When one takes the left seat he is in a position to take on a professional attitude. Speaking from my own personal experience, a pilot should try to complete all flights. Narrowing the broad statement down a bit: a pilot should *expect* to complete all flights. Merely assuming this attitude will increase the number of flights one completes in any given year. More than likely, well over 90% of all flights attempted can be completed safely.

Too many times pilots listen to the ominous forecasts of the Flight Service briefer and decide not to go. What I have found from experience is that often the weather is not nearly so unmasterable once we are out there with it as it seemed over the phone. The reason for this may be that the weather has improved or merely wasn't as horrible as the briefer tried to imply. Remember the time lag in weather reporting. What is unflyable now may be completely flyable several minutes later. This is so very true when a pilot is contemplating flight near thunderstorms.

When a pilot takes this professional attitude toward flying, it must also be tempered with good sense. The attitude to which I refer is that almost all flights should be attempted. Certainly, where a violent line of thunderstorms is approaching the airfield from the direction of one's departure, the flight should be delayed.

The flight that is begun but then comes face to face with a decision to continue or divert puts the pilot in the precarious position of having to judge his own abilities and limitations. The problem here is that abilities never grow in stature if risks aren't taken. In other words, if certain calculated risks are not taken then our ability to complete flights will remain near the beginner's level. *Calculated* risks can be taken, however, within safe operating limits. In the following pages we will discuss those margins for safety and techniques for dealing with the weather on a first-hand basis.

AIRBORNE WEATHER RADAR

In this progressive day and age where the miracle electronic breakthrough of integrated circuits and $15 hand held computers is taken for granted, radar seems like a tool from electronics' stone age. It *has* been around for a long time, but only recently has it begun to find itself in the cockpit of single engine high performance aircraft (Fig. 5-1, 5-2). This advance in itself, while not an advance for state-of-the-art radar, has made the little green-eyed giant

Fig. 5-1. The marvel of radar comes to the single-engined spectrum. Utility and safety has been increased in the IFR environment.

killer available to more pilots. Unfortunately, the higher availability in the general aviation fleet may serve only to perpetuate the mythical concepts already in wide misuse. A desperately low percentage of the total pilots flying regularly today understand certain weather radar characteristics. While these characteristics may not actually be technological deficiencies, they *are* areas of misunderstanding and false expectations.

Almost everyone is familiar with the Southern Airlines crash on April 4, 1977. The aircraft was a DC-9-31 and 72 persons died in the crash. 63 of the victims were passengers. The remaining nine were in the path of the aircraft's final breakup. Forunately, 22 passengers did survive the crash.

The National Transportation Safety Board (NTSB) reconstructed the events leading up to the accident. The flight profile disclosed that the crew had attempted to traverse an area of severe thunderstorms. As a result, the flight was subjected to heavy rain and hail. The engines ingested the hail and rain, but were unable to digest it. Both compressors stalled and heavy internal damage was incurred. Among the NTSB's conclusion was this statement: "Major contributing factors included .... the Captain's reliance on airborne weather radar for penetration of thunderstorm areas ...."

The NTSB's finding caused a wave of controversy to sweep through the aviation community. After all, *thousands* of radar sets had been sold to the air carriers and general aviation over the past twenty years. This finding was contrary to logic and accepted experience. As a matter of fact, under certain conditions radar is required under Part 121 and the new Part 135.

How then, could the accident have been attributable in part to the crew's reliance on airborne weather radar? The answer lies in *expectations* of radar. Many times, what a flight crew expects a radar installation to do is often different form the operational capabilities of the radar.

In fundamental terms, the purpose of radar is to transmit RF (radio frequency) energy ahead of the aircraft and receive returning echoes reflected back from targets in the path of the transmitted RF energy. The reflected energy from the targets is displayed on a cathode ray tube, the scope. The most significant factor influencing radar presentation is reflectivity of the target. Reflected signals from fog, dry hail, and ice crystals are very weak, at times nonexistent. The reflectivity of rain, wet snow, and large wet hail is high. Of course, hard metallic objects are the best reflectors, but weather is not made of metal, thank heavens.

As we have already discussed, ATC radar uses devices such as circular polarization to eliminate weather returns unless the precipitation is very heavy. So many times we cannot rely on ATC to help much. Such was the case for Southern's flight 242. We pick up the flight after departure.

2056:00 Huntsville Departure Control: "Southern 242, I'm painting a line of weather which appears to be moderate to uh, possible heavy precipitation, starting about uh, five miles ahead..."

Fig. 5-2. The sophistication of the single-engined aircraft pictured here rivals that of the airlines. I might add, it takes a professional attitude to fly it safely.

2056:22 (Departure): "Uh, it's painting—I got weather cutting devices on which is cutting out the, uh, precip that you're in now..."

Ground-based weather radar, on the other hand, tries to enhance weather returns. The National Weather Service's unit designated the WSR-57 operates in the 10-cm (3 GHz) wavelength range. This is a relatively low frequency as radars go. The lower frequencies penetrate thunderstorms to considerable distance before the signals are scattered or attenuated below a usable level. The wavelength, power and beam width of the WSR-57 requires a large antenna: 12 *feet* in diameter! Obviously, a unit such as this is unsuited for airborne radar use.

Engineers have solved the size problem by increasing the frequencies at which airborne radar operates. Most operate in the C-band (5.4 GHz) and X-band (9.35 GHz). The wavelength for C-band is 5cm and X-band is 3cm. These short wavelengths allow a smaller antenna that is compatible with airplane size. The trouble is that the shorter wavelength results in a performance penalty. The short frequencies are more susceptible to scattering and absorption with the end result being higher attenuation caused by atmospheric moisture when compared to ground units. Clearly, this becomes a major deficiency when large amounts of precipitation are in the "near field" of the antenna. The range suffers tremendously. In the final analysis, weather radar performance is good when viewing an area from a clear area. The radar's effectiveness and range is degraded by precipitation in direct proportion to the intensity.

There is a great amount of difference between X and C-band radars. For example, X-band is tuned to higher frequency. This makes it less effective for penetrating precipitation than C-band types. On the other side of the coin, X-band has a narrower beam width which allows greater definition of the edges and gradation of precipitation. Airborne radar performance indices assume there will only be light rainfall amounts between the antenna and storm. Light rain fall is considered to be less than 0.1 in./hr. Expected attenuation rates for both X and C-band radars are shown in Fig. 5-3.

The problem with these projected theories on how radar will be attenuated do not hold true in the real world whenever rainfall rates exceed 0.1 in./hr. X-band radar has such high susceptibility to back scatter that "blocking" of the radar scope can result. What happens is that we get badly defined returns which tend to hide any

66

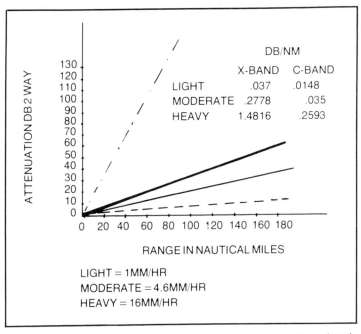

Fig. 5-3. Airborne radar performance in light to heavy rainfall conditions (courtesy of Flight Crew Magazine).

changing intensity echoes behind them. In an effort to relieve this problem, the engineers came up with a function properly known as *iso-echo-contouring* or just plain contouring. The way contouring works is by putting an upper limit on reflected RF energy. Whenever the reflected energy reaches a certain value the display is blanked electronically resulting in a contour hole. These holes are easily read by a flight crew as an area of moderate to heavy precipitation. Coincidentally, areas of heavy turbulence are generally associated with heavy rainfall.

The Southern Airways DC-9 was equipped with an X-band radar that could be operated in a normal or contour mode. Thus contour holes could be observed and avoided. Southern Airways' training guide states that contour holes should be circumnavigated by at least ten miles. The manual further explains that any weather return at a range of 75 miles or greater should be considered significant whether or not it is contouring.

Needless to say, an excursion through an indicated contour hole will result in extreme turbulence. Occasionally this happens, however, due to attenuation effects. When flying through severe

Fig. 5-4. This is a severe thunderstorm which spawned three funnel clouds and damaging hail. The hail area was at the extreme right of this picture. The coloration of the cloud in that area was a pale green. We eventually circumnavigated this monster through the light area south of the lake.

rainfall, the beam is dispersed and performance is reduced. Flying through icing can cause problems too. Radome icing causes targets to disappear and only a faint haze is displayed.

X-band radar such as the unit that Southern Airways was using is highly susceptible to attenuation whenever there is rain between the aircraft and the target. Empirical evidence suggests that X-band frequencies are more susceptible to this type of attenuation that are units utilizing lower frequencies. A surprising discovery is that the X-band may be even *more* susceptible than numerical data suggests.

To illustrate the difference between X-band and C-band, tests were conducted using heavier intervening rainfall rates of approximately 0.46 in./hr. This is considered as moderate to heavy rainfall. The contrast between the two frequency bands is substantial. Under the test conditions, the X-band unit began contouring at seven miles. The C-band unit, with significantly less dispersion, began contouring at 33 miles. Remember, that contours are electronically blanked whenever the rainfall rate reaches 0.46 in./hr.

The fact that the Southern Airways flight was already in heavy rain had to have played a large part in their misinterpretation of the radar. Here is some of the cockpit conversation as the crew made their inflight decisions.

   2105:53 (Southern 242 CVR/First Officer): "Which way we go—cross here or get out—I don't know how we get through there, Bill."

   (Captain): "I know, you're just gonna have to go on."

   (F/O): "Yeah, right across that band."

   2106:01 (CVR/Captain): "All clear left approximately right now; I think we can cut across here now."

   2106:12 (CVR/FO): "All right, here we go."

The NTSB has attempted to reconstruct the decision process associated with the conversation quoted above.

"Given the high intensity precipitation levels of the storm and comparatively short distance between the aircraft and higher intensity precipitation levels of the storm, the aircraft radar clearly should have shown a contour hole. However, the aircraft was in rain at the time, the aircraft's radar might have been affected by attenuation to the extent that when combined with the steep gradients associated with levels 3, 4, and 5 of the storm, the contour hole was distorted and interpreted by the captain as an area free from precipitation (Figs. 5-4, 5-5). The captain's comment: 'All clear left approximately right now...' at (2106:01) seems to

Fig. 5-5. This is the radar return from the storm in the previous photo. If this contour hole was down near the base of the display it would be easy to understand how a pilot could perceive the hole as an area free from precipitation. Also, note the enormity of this cell; it is longer than 30 miles.

confirm this possibility because the aircraft's course was then altered to the left, through the steep gradient, and into the highest intensity level of the storm."

Many times in flight when weather is widespread and affecting many flights in several different positions, a crew can put together a larger picture or overview in their mind from comments of other aircraft. This may have been the case with Southern 242 crew. TWA flight 584 was southbound to Atlanta and about forty miles northeast of Southern 242. They reported:

2106:38 (TWA 584): "... we paint pretty good weather one or two o'clock."

The Southern crew immediately commented:

2106:41 (CVR/FO) "He's got to be right through that hole about now."

This comment lends credibility to the theory that the Southern crew perceived the contour hole as an area of lower precipitation.

The NTSB remarks on the attenuation of radar signals in rainfall are poignant and serve as a basis for re-evaluation of training and procedures for using airborne radar.

"Scientific studies show that the X-band frequency radar is comparatively susceptible to attenuation by water vapor and precipitation. This may be particularly true when precipitation covers the antenna radome. If a pilot fails to consider this limitation, he may misinterpret the display in the process, which is a significant reason why airborne radar should *not* be used as a storm penetration aid. For maximum effectiveness, interpretation of X-band radar displays should be accomplished when the aircraft is in areas free of water vapor or precipitation."

The reason X-band is in such wide use is obvious. The higher frequency allows smaller and lighter electronic components. The higher frequency also allows higher resolution of weather returns when viewed from a distance out in the clear than does C-band. However, when observing a line of thunderstorms from maximum distance the C-band radar has the advantage. Perhaps the future holds a combination of both wavelengths in radar. That day has not arrived yet, so we must wait for technology to catch up with our needs. Until that time we would be best advised to be aware of the operational limitations of our equipment. Future training should emphasize the NTSB's findings.

As for the private pilot with no training base to go to, there is good news. There are rumblings within the aviation community that there will soon be courses in radar use and thunderstorm avoidance. These will be similar to AOPA safety seminars or weekend cram courses. With the introduction of radar into single engined aircraft, there is a need for this type of course more than ever.

AVOIDING THUNDERSTORMS

Ominous. The one word that adequately describes thunderstorms. Bulbous and threatening, they put fear in man's earliest ancestors and continue to do so today. Many storms are hazardous to ground loving persons. Mix it up with one thousands of feet above the good earth, and that ancient fear and feeling of helplessness will encompass one totally.

There is no reason, however, for us to venture into one. Not *one* good reason. Think about it. That reasoning is what should keep us well out of harm's way. Once a pilot can realize that he has no reason in the world that is strong enough to punch one, then he has virtually put himself out of danger. The most vicious lines of thunderstorms rarely endure longer than seven or eight hours. Is a business appointment, or getting to the family so important that it can't be postponed eight hours? Probably not. Even so, thunderstorm lines are rarely stationary for eight hours. If they hold together that long, they'll probably travel at least a hundred miles.

The simplest form of thunderstorm evasion is to fly up to the line and set down. The line passes overhead in a relatively short time and we fly on in the smooth air behind.

Many of you reading this book may be aspiring professional pilots. For the professional, carrying passengers for hire, setting down on the ground is rarely appealing or revenue raising. As a result, we must necessarily try to circumnavigate the storms in a safe manner. This may entail anything from making an end run to climbing up and over the saddle or dodging under. The difficulty comes when we must match the task at hand with the abilities and liabilities of our experience and aircraft. Obviously, the Captain of a Learjet has more options than the pilot-in-command of a Cessna 172.

Fundamentally, there are three types of thunderstorm situations. First, there are scattered storms that sometimes cluster. Even these clusters can sometimes band into a second type of situation: the broken line. Thirdly, and most difficult to face, is the solid line. These are generally associated with squall lines ahead of a cold front and contain the most violent and venom-spitting clouds the pilot must deal with. With practice, study, and experience all three types can be flown with a good percentage of completions— perhaps as high as 90% or 95%.

Let's begin with the easiest sort of T-storm: scattered cells. In summer, the thunderstorms known as the *airmass* type well up over every part of the country. It is this sort of situation that is most common, and that's good for us. When the cells are scattered, we have lots of room to maneuver. Many times, all we have to do is circle around the storm and join up with our airway again. Whenever the cells cluster, though, a simple circumnavigation may not work. If we can eyeball the storm and give the controller an idea of how many miles we must sidestep he may approve it without question. Remember, the controller may be painting the weather situation also. At least to some extent he is. In some cases, it may be to his benefit to issue a new clearance in an effort to reroute us. Ordinarily, it is best to accept this clearance because the route has probably been flown already by someone. They won't be sending us where everyone is getting a bad ride.

When flying around scattered cells, it is a good idea to note the direction of movement. Reaching back into our bag of knowledge from primary weather courses, we remember that the anvil top of a mature thunderstorm points in the direction it is moving. The thunderstorm that can outrun an airplane, even a modest C-150, has not been born yet. While it is true that regardless of the direction the storm is moving we should be able to go around on any side, the upwind side is the best for two reasons. First, the distance of the curcumnavigation will be shorter. Secondly, the so-called first gust pushes out in front of the storm. If for some reason we must fly fairly low and must necessarily squeeze in close, we could expose ourselves to gusty winds and a bad ride. Not to mention the dangerous inflow shelf. Many times, this wind flowing into the storm to feed the tempest will contain updrafts up to 6,500 feet per minute. There are cases where cloud seeding pilots could not lose an inch of altitude even by spinning the aircraft. That is why distance is so important in avoiding clouds.

Even on days or in areas where the cells are scattered, the sky can fill up with menacing clouds. Figure 5-6 shows an area in southern Oklahoma that was full of scattered thunderstorms, their bellies bulging with rain and hail. Our airplane was equipped with digital Collins radar and it made the task much easier. But the guy who doesn't have radar may find it much more dificult to snake his

Fig.5-6. We were level at 9,000 feet when this photo was taken. Note the lower broken layer. In order to remain in visual conditions, 9,000 feet was required.

way between cells when middle clouds are intermingling and obscuring the view ahead.

As one can see from the photograph, the situation can tend to become confusing simply due to the presence of obscuring clouds. When I shot these pictures we were level at 9,000 feet. This is contrary to most good rules of flying thunderstorms in light aircraft. Then why were we there? Examine the photo closely. It will become evident that there was a broken layer in the 3,000 to 4,000-foot range. Plainly, thunderstorms are difficult to avoid when the plane is embedded in a cloud layer. This wasn't a warm front situation where a pilot can expect to be fighting embedded thunderstorms; these clouds were part of the inflow into these powerful thunderstorms. Flying low could only do two things for us—*both* negative. We would get moderate turbulence from the inflow and obscure our vision.

Regardless, if we have airborne radar or not, the visual plays a tremendously important part in evading the bruisers. Being flexible to each thunderstorm day is another ingredient for flight safety. From a distance, one can have a good overall view of how the thunderstorms are locating themselves and their direction of movement. As we approach these marauding titans, they seem to cloak themselves in shrouds of clouds. Obviously, their ability to camouflage themselves makes the task even more trying. When

73

Fig. 5-7. The radar shows plenty of room to maneuver around the cells shown in the previous photo.

these storms are of the scattered type there are no saddles as such between them. On this particular day, 9,000 feet got us up out of the soup and able to look around.

The airborne radar was quite a help. It outlined the precip areas so that we could skirt them and squeeze in between them. Figure 5-7 showing the radar (though of poor quality due to turbulence) depicts the same storm in the previous photo. The storm was in the far right side of the picture. We avoided the precip area by about four miles. We were barely able to stay clear of clouds, but I feel that is the most important thing to do in this situation. I must point out that we were IFR, but staying VFR was of the essence. Although in the area near this colossus was a possible inflow shelf and even hail dropping out from under the anvil top, the ride was good. Even though it seemed like violation of good operating rules to avoid thunderstorms by *five* miles, the reason becomes clear why we were where we were.

Examine Fig. 5-8. Taken only a few seconds after the first two, it is obvious now that our room to maneuver was minimal. The first photo (Fig. 5-6) was taken straight out the wind screen in the direction of travel. This particular photo was taken out of the left cockpit, noting the prop. In the photograph there seems to be about five to seven miles to the cauliflower-looking storm conspicuously growing to greater magnitude. Why then were we four miles close to one and seven miles distant to another? Why not split the distance, say five and one-half miles from each? Simply, the best way looked to be where we went. Remember, the area was full of clouds coming from the surrounding square miles being sucked into these behemoths. Remaining visual is one's best insurance for getting the best ride and staying out of hail or precip. Just behind the prop is a towering cumulus cloud that was growing and obscuring the view ahead. We easily slipped around it and maintained VFR.

All this time the controller was very helpful. We were passing through the sectors of two different approach controls. Sometimes working with approach controls is a better situation than working with "center" controllers. The reason for this, I believe, is that the approach controllers at small to medium size installations don't mind twisting knobs to provide weather information. Both Altus and Shepherd AFB controllers regularly turn off the "moving target indicators" and "circular polarization" to provide as much weather avoidance as possible. Whenever traffic gets heavy, though, traffic separation becomes the most important function of the controller. On this particular day in April, all the controllers were bending over backward to honor our request for higher, then lower, then higher just to remain visual.

Flying around thunderstorms is seldom simple once coverage grows to 40% to 50%. The pilots who were high aloft that day had

Fig. 5-8. In this, the third photo of the series, the airplane is squeezing between a cell on the left which was *not* depicted on the radar due to its location.

similar problems to the ones we encountered below. Large thunderstorms are rarely just one cumulonimbus cloud. Once the giant is maturing, clouds of all shapes and sizes cluster around like the pilot fish swimming alongside a shark. At the high altitudes the anvil top blows off and creates a stratus deck for possibly hundreds of miles. These decks pose the same sort of problem that a lower deck would to a single-engine lightplane pilot. At the high flight levels the difference between cruise speed and stall speed is a razor-thin line. Any turbulence that is strong enough to cause movement of the flight controls could lead to a substantial problem. Thus, the high fliers prefer to remain visual as well.

Most stormy days, the task is easier in the flight levels. When the tops are in the 30,000-foot to 40,000-foot range and the upper winds are relatively light, the difficulty is reduced to simply driving between pylons of turbulent air. Difficult situations do occur, however, when a jet must descend for landing into an area of scattered embedded thunderstorms. The radar paints the storms, but they are well below. Such was the situation as we arrived in the Greensboro, N.C. area one summer evening. Watching out the windows we intently observed the lightning, revealing the location of each cell and then correlating it to the radar. The flashes of lightning looked like cherry bombs exploding in a stock tank in the dark—an unusual sight sensation shared by relatively few people in this world. After we entered the clouds, all decisions would be based on radar returns. It's times like these when I wish we were already down low. Yet the Captain deftly slid the three—holer in between a short line of cells to the north and two isolated cells to the south.

Encountering only light chop, I had to wonder why we didn't swing wide to south and skirt all the cells. It had to be years of experience of flying into this particular airport that made the difference. The Captain had a mental image in his mind of exactly where the runway threshold was in relation to the cells. Wagering the speed of the spry 727 against that of a lumbering storm, the route we took turned out to be both expedient and smooth. He made it seem easy. It wasn't.

Many times, I've been approaching a line of storms in mid-summer and have looked up to see a silver dot streaking through the saddle above. The crew, having done nothing more difficult than changing lanes on a busy freeway, was free from the beast.

Earlier we mentioned there were three types of flying

situations that thunderstorms throw at us. We have just discussed the scattered type. The other two are broken and solid lines of storms. Both types of lines *can* be flown safely although the margin for error is much less than for isolated cells.

We will be continuing with the series of photographs we started a few pages back. Once we worked our way through the malange of scattered cells, the situation got worse. *Much* worse. There was a wave pattern beginning to develop. The scattered storms behind were quickly clustering to become a line. Ahead of us though, a line had already formed. For a hundred miles or more the bad news was that the average tops were 54,000 feet. The high fliers began wishing they were down low. There was no place to go through, up high, for several hundred miles. Down low, *we* were beginning to wish this was our day off.

If you look at Fig. 5-9 you can see our dilemma. No longer was 9,000 feet going to work. In a matter of minutes we would put our nose into the belly of an intense level six (the most severe) thunderstorm. The clouds were now strung out from a few hundred feet AGL to halfway to heaven.

It has been discovered and studied that the level of least turbulence in a cell is at or below 4,000 feet AGL. The reason for this is that updrafts have not had sufficient distance to accelerate to maximum levels. The downdrafts tend to fan out near the surface.

Fig. 5-9. As the cells grew around and ahead of us, it became apparent that 9,000 would put us into the belly of one of the storms sooner or later. The decision was made to descend.

77

More than once pilots have been pushed downward (unable to outclimb the downdraft), to be reprieved from the upward rush of the ground in the nick of time.

At this point our radar became clobbered with storm cells. There was one main line and ahead, but before we got there we had to weave almost drunkenly between scattered cells. The radar was now so full and painting such a limited picture overall we had to query the controller. Upon doing this we asked if there was any clear routing to DFW airport. He spouted off some unfamiliar list of victor airways and intersections, causing us to reach for the enroute chart in the flight bag. It was evident that 9,000 feet wouldn't work no matter *which* way we went. We requested 4,000.

Down we went through the towering cu you see in the photo. Our vision through the windscreen became obscured by clouds most of the time. We began to rely on the Collins WXR - 250 to pull us through. The cumulus gave us the usual ride—rougher than a cob. By the time we reached 4,000 feet we had the new route "lined out" and were beginning to decide on what our alternatives were to insure safety. It looked as though there was a small break in the line of weather just east of our route.

4,000 feet wasn't doing the job. It was time to request flight at the MEA. 3,000 feet was approved and again we were in visual conditions. Indeed it appeared there was no precipitation at our 11 o'clock position. The request for deviation was approved and off we ventured for clear air. As we approached the gap there was little room to squeeze through, but it was adequate. Admittedly, one would like more room to maneuver.

Let's check the final photograph of this series, Fig. 5-10. It was taken about 50 miles into the storm area from where we first encountered scattered cells. This storm was part of the line that was topping 54,000 feet. It is also part of what would be considered a solid line. Notice the roll cloud at the bottom of this muscular giant. This roll cloud means one thing: treacherous turbulence! My experience has shown that an aircraft can skirt these clouds quite close without getting a ripple. On this day we paralleled the cloud within three miles and got a good ride.

Squirting through the opening, we popped into the clear area ahead of the line. The rest of the ride to the airport was uneventful. As we viewed the scene behind us, the clouds glowered a magnificent dark gray. Certainly, it gave the appearance of being a no-man's land; unnavigable. But such are appearances, especially when the transition of such weather situations is one's profession.

Fig. 5-10. Now level at 3,000 feet, we squeezed between two more cells and out into the open. Note the roll cloud at the base of this storm. I have a standing rule *not* to punch anything like this!

The one thing I *don't* want to be accused of is encouraging low time pilots to fly into the face of fierce odds. A thunderstorm's fury is unpredictable, but in the series of photographs I have illustrated some methods that work for me and my crew time after time. Although it seems that we were pushing on regardless of the consequences, nothing could be further from the truth. Always, *always*, leave yourself an out or an airport to retreat to. As we entered the area of scattered thunderstorm we had several airports to divert to, namely, Altus and Lawton, Oklahoma Municipal Airports. Once we were ahead of the scattered stuff, but faced punching the line, our retreat point was Wichita Falls Municipal standing clear under beaming sunny skies.

The inflight decision to continue or retreat is rarely black or white. Let's talk about a few of the things to be considered in making a decision when flying around thunderstorms.

If the storms are scattered we should examine how much room we have to maneuver around them. Three miles should be a minimum distance if we can remain clear of clouds in visual conditions. If these conditions exist one can cruise on in relative safety. If one can't remain visual, than five miles from the storm should be the absolute minimum distance. One can keep this distance by one of three ways: onboard radar, ground ATC radar,

Fig. 5-11. Take a good look at this storm and the following photo of the radar. There can be a great size discrepancy. The storm is larger than the echo.

or eyeballing the main column of the storm prior to cloud entry (Fig. 5-11, 5-12). Basically, if these guidelines cannot be followed, the situation is stepping over the margin of safety and the attempt should be aborted. Also, remember that any time that the flight must enter clouds, the chances for turbulence and an uncomfortable ride are greatly increased.

The decision to fly through a line of boomers, whether broken or a solid line, takes a great deal of consideration. First, there is *no* reason to risk anything. Yet, there is also no reason to sit on the ground a hundred miles away and assume we cannot fly through it or around it or at worst just make some progress up to it and stop. When coming face to face with a line, decisions should be made early. Airborne radar can quickly spot the holes or breaks in the line. Go for the largest holes closest to your route and ask for deviations early. If you don't have radar, query the controller early and go through where the others are unless a better way is clearly visible.

Once we are next to the line, we must first decide if our altitude is best. If one is flying light aircraft (non-pressurized), then we should be low enough to remain visual. On the other hand, if we are flying high performance pressurized aircraft we may want to cross at a saddle. Interpretation of the rate the cloud is building at the saddle is important (Fig. 5-13). Our altitude should be well above it, remaining visual all the while.

The pilot with little experience should abort the attempt if he cannot remain in visual conditions. If VFR can be maintained I would encourage a pilot to go for it! Transiting safely through will give a pilot confidence in his ability to pick a good hole and safely navigate through it. The feeling of accomplishment is to be treasured. Even when remaining visual, be sure to reduce airspeed in anticipation of turbulence. Be sure to use gust penetration speed, maneuvering speed, or lower if the airplane is at less than maximum gross weight—which it should be. The speed reduction should be accomplished about a mile from coming abeam with the nearest clouds associated with the storm. Once the turbulence associated with the transition has subsided, cruise power can be resumed.

When flying between cells related in a line of storms, cloud penetration sometimes is inevitable—at least, if we are to complete the flight. It is advised that one *not* try this unless he or she has ridden through similar weather conditions before with a competent experienced pilot. Once again, radar makes all the difference. Either airborne or ATC radar should be used to line the aircraft up in the center of the hole. Gust penetration speed should be used. If radar is unavailable because of our low altitude (we should ideally be within 4,000 feet of the surface), or we do not have airborne equipment—eyeball it. We must necessarily line

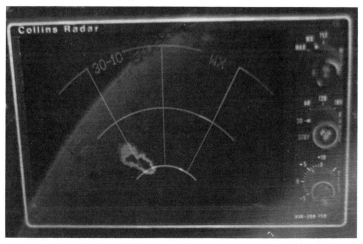

Fig. 5-12. Although of poor quality, this picture still shows that most times the echo is smaller than the cloud. The problem is that when we cut too close to a storm by using radar alone, we may venture into the cloud and extreme turbulence by accident. Try to stay visual.

ourselves up outside the clouds because turns are extremely difficult and hazardous once in turbulence.

The eyeball method is undesirable whenever the line is several miles thick. Many times, thunderstorm lines can be as much as 60 miles wide with cells staggered throughout. The result is that eyeballing it, going in, doesn't do much good a few miles in. The best method of success in this instance is to try and find an altitude between cloud layers. The storm centers can be avoided handily as long as the cloud layers don't merge. Of course, this is impossible at times and always easier said than done.

Early in my flying career, I had the opportunity to become a copilot for a freight-carrying airline. One of the most nerve-racking experiences I lived through was flying through a thunderstorm line which had been plaguing us all week. It was associated with a slow-moving cold front and we had to cross it back-to-front, then on the return front-to-back each night of this particular work week. Having been through the line several times already didn't make us relish the task. We'd been belittled, angered and beaten by this string of storms until we were considering resignation and another occupation.

The Beech 18 Turbine was droning towards Chicago inbound from Pittsburgh and the brilliant lightning display ahead was testimony of what was to come. It was about 4 o'clock in the morning and we were tired as always. The flashing stung our eyes and one of Chicago Center's finest stung us as well. The controller said the line was 40 to 60 miles thick and was solid for a 120 miles in either direction from us. The line was massive in length as well as depth. We had no onboard radar and the controller was as much help.

"Great Western 658, what I'm painting is solid and I see no holes."
We queried further, "Is *anyone* going through *anywhere*?"
Chicago: "I haven't had anybody try it in a couple of hours."
GW 658: "Which way looks the best from here?"
Chicago: "It all looks bad, I have no suggestions. You are free to deviate any direction you wish."

Great. No radar help of any kind and the look on the Captain's face told me we were going to put our nose into it anyway. Soon he gave me instructions to watch for lightning pulses and that we would veer away from areas of greatest intensity and most flashes. It was odd that normally we descended to 4,000 feet to get ready for the ride. Tonight was different. I guess it was instinct, because

Fig. 5-13. This photo was taken in the area of the storm that spawned three funnel clouds featured on an earlier page. This picture depicts the retreat in the opposite direction. As you can see, the retreat has only one hole and the clouds are building there. Leave yourself an out and pay attention to what is going on *behind* you in case you must exit.

there certainly was no visual information suggesting that our 6,000 feet was the altitude we should use. The hair was standing up on the back of my neck, bristling like a cat's as we came abeam of a storm on each side.

A stratus deck began to slide underneath us and seconds later we were safely past the two huge columns of cloud. The scene inside the line was eerie. We were enveloped by clouds above, below and alongside. In essence, it was like driving down a hallway or a boulevard lined with large trees. The lightning was making the trip more like a ride down the Las Vegas strip. Everytime it would flash, we'd discuss whether it was cloud to cloud or a cell shooting its electrical messages to the ground. The cells weren't easily identified the way the lightning was bouncing around in that hall of clouds.

The controller with all of his help finally told us we had about another twenty miles to go. We veered this way until we saw a cell in front of us then veered that way to miss seemingly countless masses of sullen, swollen demons. The old 18 was still between layers and droning along contentedly. Her nonchalance seemed to say that she'd seen all this before. Her copilot *hadn't*. The last 20 miles disappeared behind us and the constant flashing gave way to the steady glow of Chicago's millions, freshly washed to start a new day.

Looking over at the Captain it was easy to see the amazement on his face. The stern, straight-ahead, all business gaze was gone and the twinkle in his eyes said it all. Neither of us could believe that we'd just flown sixty miles of nature's worst and never hit a ripple. Not a bump! The ride was satiny smooth. That's got to be some sort of near psychic feat.

Certainly, I don't recommend anyone fly this way. Yet back in the early, DC-3 days, airline crews did it all the time. I don't want to do it again, but I wouldn't have missed it for anything in the world.

AS DIFFERENT AS DAY AND NIGHT

In the ranks of pilots who fly thunderstorms regularly year after year, there is a controversy. That argument is whether it is easiest to fly the devils in the daytime or at night. One side argues that at night the lightning lights up the cells and thus they are easier to avoid. The other side says that in close-knit lines of storm, the lightning is reflected off *all* the clouds and that actual detection of the storm cell is vague at best. The truth lies somewhere in between. However, after giving this subject some thought I came to realize that out of the last three years, I have been rebuffed and unable to punch lines of storms only three times. All three times were at night. Another interesting fact was that there was only one cancellation each year.

The greatest problem with flying thunderstorms after dark is dealing with the flowing skirts of cloud around their bases. The foremost reason for turning away are lines of storms. As we have already discussed, staying visual is the best way to avoid thunderstorms. Some may ask if flying IFR isn't flying in the clouds. Regardless of whether we have filed IFR on a flight or not, the best method to avoid thunderstorms is to *stay in visual conditions.* The dark makes this a formidable task.

Scattered thunderstorms *are* just as easy to circumnavigate at night as in the daytime. In fact, the argument that the lightning makes them easy to avoid is valid. The techniques that we discussed in the last section on navigating broken or solid lines are altered in the dark. In the spring, thunderstorm bases are generally closer to the ground than their summer cousins. This time of year makes the task at night that much more difficult. Whereas before, during daylight, we could eyeball the bases and make a good general guess as to what altitude would be clear below, darkness changes that. One reason is that the bases are not clearly visible even if they become illuminated by lightning charges. Thus, descending to the MEA, for example, may just run the aircraft face to face with a roll cloud.

There is a much greater need for airborne storm detection equipment during darkness than during daylight. When flying areas of storms in the evening I resign myself to the fact that I will inevitably fly into some clouds. In some ways there is a psychological advantage. One expects to run into the clouds and come fairly close to the cells. Thus, much of the anxiety can be channeled into purely exercising logic and avoiding the storms by the maximum distance possible.

Another possible advantage to flying around storms at night is that they are generally dying out. Thus, intensities are not what they might be. This won't hold true for frontal situations, but *may* for airmass type thunderstorms. Flying north out of Boise, Idaho after midnight on a mail route, I saw a flash of lightning ahead. My jaw started working as the adrenalin began to run through my veins. Avoiding storms in the mountains was far from one of my favorite pastimes. Twenty miles later I was looking for the storm. Finally, I spotted a puff of cloud ahead. Nothing to worry about, though. My course took me directly under it. It was dissipating fast. The Aztec scooted underneath with one little thump. The thunderstorm had died before my eyes. The flash of lightning I saw must have been its last hurrah.

In the evening and early morning hours very few pilots are aloft. As a result, the airwaves on controller frequencies are conspicuously quiet. The result is that controllers are able, if they are willing, to devote more time to each aircraft. In sectors where weather is a major factor in handling traffic most controllers go out of their way to provide vectors around weather showing on their displays. This is a definite benefit to flying at night and a great aid in getting around thunderstorms.

The other side of the coin is flying around weather in the daylight. This is *my* preference to be sure. All the techniques we discussed in the previous section are available and viable. It provides great peace of mind to know that one has many alternatives available. For instance, in the daylight one can ascertain how long and well developed a line of storms is. At night one can only infer how developed they are by the frequency of lightning associated with them. During the day, also, it might be easier to see the end of a line and make an end run, whereas at night we might decide to pound on through.

The major difference, though, is being able to see the bases. In tornado alley, where most of my flying is done, many times the best way to avoid the monsters and still complete the flight is by ducking under as we described and illustrated earlier. When the lines of storms are of the level four to six range this can be the only way to complete the flight.

A pilot should remember that level six is the most severe of storms and severe storms are normally associated with a front or an upper level disturbance. Simply, this means they will be in bands.

So there you are, the day versus night controversy. Fly the storms the same day and night the best you can. The need to alter techniques will be apparent. Above all, *don't* fly too far beyond your personal limitations; *do* be bold enough to tackle new situations. The main thing not to do is don't deliberately fly into a storm cell. It is possible a pilot could develop ulcers in just a few minutes of that kind of treatment.

PUTTING A DECISION ON ICE

Flying through a cold front is difficult in winter. Cold fronts have steep frontal slopes and the significance this has for the aviator is that weather can change abruptly. Approaching a cold front from the south side. the weather may be sunny and smooth. Once in the area of the cold front, however, the clouds tend to stack up quickly. The layers may go from near the surface to well above the tropopause. Lifting action is associated with all fronts, but a cold front produces the most instability. Thus, the heaviest turbulence and heaviest precipitation are associated with cold fronts.

As we just mentioned, in the area of the cold front, clouds stack up quickly. It has been found that moderate precipitation requires a cloud thickness of about 4,000 feet. This is notable and important to those who operate light aircraft. Transitioning through a cold front may be difficult because of ice in the clouds. If the ice is in moderate precipitation, then cloud thicknesses may preclude any possibility of climbing to a between-layers condition.

With moderate precipitation falling, careful monitoring of the outside air temperature is compulsory. When precip is moderate, ice buildup on the airframe can be severe. Therefore, choice of altitudes can be critical.

We know that cold fronts lift warm air aloft. We also know that the frontal slope is steep. Therefore, to climb and stay in warmer air in a cold front would be futile in a lightplane. In order to escape icing in a cold frontal situation, one must weigh the facts. If ice is already accumulating on the airframe, a climb may be out of the question. This may be due either to an already high operating altitude where little excess horsepower is left for climbing or to the destruction of lift by the ice already present. In such a situation a descent should be begun as soon as possible. Hopefully, either an ice-free altitude will be found below, or the descent can be continued to a precautionary approach and landing made at the nearest airport.

Under some icing conditions a climb is possible. In cold front conditions, don't expect warmer air above. Expect colder air—so cold that freezing no longer occurs. An outside temperature below 15 degrees Fahrenheit at least, will be necessary. Also, the airframe will need to be chilled sufficiently so that frost does not form.

On the positive side of things, cold front activity often is not very wide. All this means is that the problems of icing may not last the entire trip. This is *not* to say that a pilot should continue onward foolishly in the hope that the sky will soon be blue ahead.

The easiest way for a pilot to determine if he has passed through the cold front is to watch the temperature gauge; a significant temperature drop will be noticed once through the front. Also, a wind correction to the right will be needed. This applies to any front no matter what the direction of flight. In the northern hemisphere, a right-hand wind correction is needed after frontal passage.

Almost anyone can recognize a cold front in the winter. The blustery winds and snows that have the audacity to cover our cars and homes are all part of it. However, recognition of the warm front may be one of the finer arts of piloting an aircraft cross-country.

No two warm fronts are the same. The combination of dangers of structural icing and low ceilings and visibilities almost never present themselves in a manner that makes a "go or no-go" decision easy. For that matter, a 180 degree turn usually is not an easy decision at which to arrive. As a result, the cold weather aviator must arm himself with some basic tools that will enable him to soar through the ragged wisps of clouds and decide whether to continue or land.

As compared to cold fronts, warm fronts have shallow frontal slopes. They are caused by warmer air overtaking and riding up over the trailing edge of cooler air. The shallow slope causes widespread cloudiness and low visibilities, often for hundreds of miles.

Cirrus clouds are the vanguard of the warm front. They appear where the warm air has been forced aloft up the slope of the cold air to an altitude of 20,000 feet or more. The average slope of a warm front is one percent or less. Thus, the first high clouds may be found as far as 500 miles or more in advance of the front. Approaching a warm front from the north side, a pilot will see clouds in a predetermined sequence. If we are familiar with this sequence, we can predict the changes that follow. The first clouds encountered are cirrus, followed by cirrostratus, altostratus, and nimbostratus in that order. Precipitation may begin about 300 miles from the front.

The warm sector, which we mentioned earlier, is the wedge of air to the south of the warm front. The wind changes from an east or southeasterly direction. The temperature will rise and, again, we will need a wind correction to the right after passing the front. If the warm sector is moist and the air unstable, there are likely to be snow showers if surface temperatures permit. Low ceilings and visibilities may persist after frontal passage in an inversion type effect with low cloud tops.

There are two sides to every frontal system. When considering a warm front, a pilot must be alert. From the south side, a warm front looks very much like a cold front and a VFR pilot would not likely be enticed to penetrate the system. On the north side, however, a VFR pilot flying from good weather may be tempted to continue because the first signs look harmless enough. In the winter, however, warm fronts are freezing rain or drizzle producers. The rain will usually start coming down miles before the front where the pilot is flying under an umbrella of altostratus or altocumulus. Depending on the temperature aloft, icing may become a problem from the freezing drizzle. If temperatures are quite cold, then light snow will substitute for the freezing drizzle. The visibilities will then become low, and IFR becomes mandatory to complete a flight.

The IFR pilot may have it made for a while if he is traveling toward the front from the north. But as the frontal slope gets nearer the earth there is less time for the warm precipitation to be changed to a solid. Then, until the front passes, it becomes rain even though temperatures remain low at the lower altitudes. What the IFR pilot must do is climb to get on top of the frontal slope where all the air is warm and above freezing. This is usually, but not always, possible.

Warm fronts produce predominantly rime ice due to the stratiform clouds. As the pilot flies toward the front, though, cumuliform clouds are encountered which can cause severe clear icing. If the temperature at the surface is as cold as 14 degrees Fahrenheit and the warm front is close at hand, icing may be expected from within 300 to 400 feet of the surface to above 15,000 feet in the cumuliform clouds. This leaves a large part of the general aviation fleet on the ground.

A low pressure center during the winter months is a blizzard builder. The warm moist air is pumped up over the top of the cold air and around to the northeast side. The moist air reaches its dewpoint and begins to fall into the cold air below, resulting in snow at the lower altitudes. Beware the northeast side of a low in the winter; this area is frequently the best for heavy snow accumulations. As the front occludes, the storm gains its greatest fury. On these days, it is best not to go at all.

Now, let's get down to the meat of the subject of avoiding ice. The hard thing about learning to fly in icing conditions is there are no rules of thumb. Some old pros always say to climb, but in light aircraft, a climb is not always possible. So there goes *that* rule. If there is a secret to flying ice, it is the combination of a good preflight briefing and experience. No one is born with experience, so at some point in time we are forced to get our feet wet.

The key to knowing where to go to get out of ice can be found in the winds aloft forecast. Along with wind direction and velocities, temperatures are estimated. It is normal for the temperatures to decrease with an increase in altitude; but, unfortunately for those of us who fly in the slop a lot, that isn't always the case. Many items, inversions form and warmer temperatures can be found. Temperature inversions can fall anywhere in the atmosphere. They are most likely to be found in the winter, however, between 4,000 and 9,000 feet.

The question is simple—whenever an inversion is predicted, what do we do about ice? Of course, the temperature above the inversion must be above freezing, or right at it, to do us any good. Even when a pilot has anti-icing and de-icing equipment, he should endeavor to find an altitude free of ice.

Often, ice is associated with flying in clouds. We spoke of rime ice earlier. Rime ice is a fine granular ice that appears mild-white in color. It usually builds forward into the slipstream. Knowing what kind of ice is attacking the airframe can be useful in determining how to avoid it. For example, rime ice is associated with stratiform clouds. Stratiform clouds are typically layered and not excessively thick under most circumstances. A haven from ice, then, can sometimes be found between those stratus layers.

Let's say you are cruising at an altitude of 5,000 feet. At this altitude, the clouds are solid, and hard-core instrument flying is required. On the climb up to 5,000 feet you topped one layer and climbed into the one you are operating in now. The temperature aloft forecast shows an inversion above freezing in the area of 6,000 feet. What is the best way out of the ice?

In a situation like this, a climb would not be foolhardy. Seven thousand feet will put you above the inversion in warmer air, probably, where there will be no ice. Also, since the tops of inversions are frequently the tops of cloud decks, any precipitation encountered at 7,000 feet would not stick to the plane. Another point in favor of climbing first is knowing we can fly between layers below 5,000 feet—the proverbial "ace in the hole."

On days when no inversion above is expected, the same choice can be made. If there are no pilot reports of tops in the area, I usually try to find them. If the total cloud decks can be topped, we can fly fat, dumb and happy in the sun. During climbouts, always remember where the layer tops were since some days it is the only place to go.

Clear ice is not so easy to handle. It is usually formed by precipitation or flight through cumuliform clouds. It is the nature of clear ice to have a high rate of accretion, often near the tops of these clouds. Because of this it is imperative to arrive at a decision quickly. A short climb, a change of 1,000 feet in altitude, may free the plane of the condition. Also, it is often clear above the tops of this type of clouds. If you are near the top of the deck and clear conditions exist a short distance above, the light will be intense from the sun. A climb should be initiated at once and the condition will vanish.

On the other hand, if the clear ice is due to precipitation you'll know it. The sleet and rain slamming against the windscreen is warning enough. This type of icing usually turns out to be the most severe. Therefore, avoidance precautions should be taken at once. Many times, the best place to go is *down*—down to the nearest airport for a cup of coffee and a call to the family.

If a plane is equipped with anti-ice and de-ice equipment, the battle will go more smoothly because a pilot can spend more time looking for the right altitude. It is easy to see that de-icing equipment can take a great deal of stress off the pilot. It is well worth the money.

What some pilots may not know is there is a technique for using de-icing equipment to maximum advantage.

First, if the plane starts picking up ice, begin action *immediately* in selecting another altitude. All anti-ice gear should be turned "on" if it wasn't prior to entering the cloud. Among anti-ice gear are the hot props, pitot heat, and electric windshield. This equipment will do much to prolong the flight at the initial cruising altitude if, for some reason, a change cannot be initiated right away due to terrain or conflicting traffic.

Secondly, let the ice build on the airfoils until ¾-inch to one inch is present on the leading edge. If expansion boots are used too early, the end result may be like not having boots at all. If the ice is not of sufficient thickness, the boots will not be able to pop it off. Sometimes, if the boots are exercised prematurely, they will expand the ice outward leaving a hollow space underneath. The ice will then continue to accumulate but will not be removed by further expansions because each expansion is the same size.

Once the ice has been broken off, let the ice accumulation begin again. Of course, continue efforts to find an ice-free altitude. Always be careful to allow about an inch to accumulate before exercising the boots.

Some expansion boot systems have an automatic cycle function. Unless ice accretion is occurring at an alarming rate, always operate the boots manually. Automatic expansion every 20 or 30 seconds is too much and may result in one of the conditions of non-performance mentioned above.

If you are new to flying ice or new at flying a twin-engine aircraft in ice, there are some sounds you can expect to hear that can be alarming. The most common noise is that of ice slinging off the props. The loud bang can be heard even when wearing a headset. Passengers should be warned that they might hear this sound. Another sound comes from the long wire ADF antenna that runs from the top of the cabin to the vertical stabilizer. Once this wire accumulates ice it will begin to vibrate with a low pitch. The low frequency flutter is more of a vibration that a sound, but you'll know what it is when you hear it.

Ice accumulation on a twin is like a visit to a house of horrors. The groans and creaks of the airplane are unusual and they can be very disturbing. Regardless of the type of aircraft, icing should be considered dangerous. The best time to do something about ice is *right away*. With immediate action, navigation through icy areas can be achieved with regularity and safety. The problems of icing in the winter can be handled much more easily than those of the thunderstorms of summer. *Cold Weather Flying*, TAB book No. 2273, is recommended for further reading.

Chapter 6
Partial Panel

The old airplane creaked along basking in the sunlight as the fuel gauges were clicking the miles off. The destination was close at hand and the crew was about to leave the pale blue sky above for the steel gray deck below.

"Get the cat out of his cage," the Captain commanded.

"What about the duck?" asked the First Officer.

"Wait till we get well into the clouds; then throw him out."

"Well, there we go. We're in the clouds now," retorted the First Officer.

What are these guys doing? It resembles a scene from "Abbot and Costello Join the Air Farce." Well friends, they are flying instruments the original no-gyro way. It is known as the Cat and Duck Method, made famous in the early days of hangar aviation. It almost sounds like a viable concept. Certainly, a cat always lands on its feet and tends to remain upright. And, any duck worth a quack wouldn't fly in lousy weather. The method was to watch the cat and see which way he was leaning to keep the plane upright. The duck was to be tossed out the window to commence the instrument approach portion, and then followed to the ground, as its natural instincts were to get on the ground.

The method had very little success. Try as they may, the cat would go to sleep or roll on its back for its tummy to be rubbed. Legend has it that the duck wouldn't allow itself to be tossed into the slop; it wasn't going to fly in that sort of weather starting from *anywhere*. As a result the C & D Method has fallen into disuse in recent times. Holdovers from the past still exist, though: I have one copilot that is so nostalgia-ridden that he still flies with a rubber duck.

The term *partial panel* has replaced the C & D Method as the term meaning no gyro instruments available for flight reference. Somewhere in every instrument pilot's learning curriculum, the instructor introduces partial panel. Partial panel always represents, at least at first, total frustation. Having all the "good" references robbed from one's scan causes the plane to begin various aberrations as attitude is maintained by the ancient combo of needle, ball and airspeed.

According to Murphy's Law, in any field of endeavor many things can go wrong. In the field of instrument flight, the possible combinations of things that can go wrong are incredible. However, there are only 13 likely combinations ranging from single instrument failure to total system failure. Regardless of the degree of disruption, none of them should be relegated to the role of driving the final nail in a pilot's coffin.

In this chapter we will ignore all the related systems such as navigation, communication and auto-pilots and concentrate on the cardinal six. Those instruments are the airspeed indicator (ASI); attitude indicator (ADI), sometimes known as the artificial horizon; altimeter (ALT); turn and bank (T & B); directional gyro (DG); and the vertical speed indicator (VSI).

First, we should review which instruments represent movement about which aircraft axes. There are three axes: lateral (pitch), longitudinal (roll), and vertical (yaw). Lateral control is maintained by reference to the ADI, ASI, ALT, VSI, power, and trim. The longitudinal or roll axis is reflected in monitoring the ADI, DG, T & B as well as the magnetic compass. The yaw or vertical axis is represented by only the ball in the turn and bank indicator.

All of the above instruments must have an energy source to make them function properly or at all. The vacuum pump is ordinarily engine-driven. The attitude indicator and directional gyro depend upon the vacuum pump. The altimeter, airspeed indicator and vertical speed indicator are directly responsible to the proper operation of the pitot-static system. The only electrically operated gyro on most general aviation aircraft is the turn and bank or turn coordinator. Almost strangely, there are two components that do not depend on any other energy source except inertia and they are the compass and ball.

If we think about it only one instrument from each axis is necessary to maintain control of the aircraft. That means we can do without several instruments. For example, all the basic maneuvers such as straight and level, climbs, descents and turns can be done with just an ADI and ball. What this means is that four separate instrument failures would have to occur to deprive a pilot of the necessary references on both the longitudinal and lateral axes. The vertical axis (yaw) should always be intact unless the instrument face is broken. All this makes the possibility of individual failures becoming catastrophic quite remote. When gross failures *do* occur, they are usually the result of system failures.

INDIVIDUAL INSTRUMENT FAILURE

In my years of flying there is one instrument that has failed more than the rest. It is the attitude indicator (ADI). It is also the one instrument that most of us favor. When it fails, our main reference is gone. On close inspection though, we can see that its loss is mainly an inconvenience rather than a tragedy. In instrument training, the first failure your instructor probably simulated was the failure of the artificial horizon. Hence, the failure is probably a familiar one. For pitch information we must shift our scan to the VSI, ALT, or ASI. The airspeed is probably the quickest to react and thus will provide the most use. The vertical speed indicator will help, but its inherent lag makes it of little use as far as I am concerned. It does help to maintain a constant pitch attitude once one has been established. Still, the ASI is more adept at this function.

The altimeter also indicates the trend that the plane is going through: up or down. One facet of use that many instrument flight instructors fail to explore with students is that the altimeter is a good indicator of the rate-of-change. It doesn't indicate a rate as does the VSI, but the rate at which the large hand is moving is very indicative of the severity of the nose attitude.

Whenever we have ADI failure we should remember to do two things, one of them immediately. First, disconnect any navaids that derive information from the attitude indicator. Secondly, we should cover the face of that dial. Even though we would consciously realize that that instrument is inoperative, it is still habit to correct everytime we scan past it. I must confess I have jerked the controls after an ADI failure, thinking we were in a steep turning climb. It is an uncomfortable thing to do to passengers and is very disconcerting. A passenger's faith can be shaken or washed away by such an event.

After we have eliminated the failed ADI from our scan we will necessarily spend more time looking at the turn and bank indicator. We should remember that this instrument is *interpretive* rather than *symbolic*. In other words, the attitude is *not* depicted. It is, more accurately, measuring the rate at which the aircraft is turning. A good rule of thumb to recall in times of need is that full scale needle deflection comes in the neighborhood of 45 degrees in most light aircraft (realizing, of course, that speed directly influences the needle's reaction). But, it may give us something to hold on to, if we need that sort of reassurance.

When the airspeed indicator fails for some reason, flying the plane back to the ground can be tough. This is a top of the line instrument failure and luckily it doesn't happen very often. Nothing can put a lump in a pilot's throat quicker than to see the ASI winding down through stall speed. The natural reaction is to force the nose down, but a quick glance at the altimeter and VSI shows that nothing is happening. From here we are faced with shooting an approach without the instrument that infers information about our angle of attack. Scary!

The first thing to do after discovery of our misfortune is to cover the wayward instrument up. This should help in restraining us from chasing the VSI through the sky with roller coaster-like attitude changes. The next thing we should realize is that the ASI is a luxury in level flight. We rarely refer to it in our normal scan while we are trucking cross-country. Cruise-climbs and descents should pose no problem, either. Just adjust the power and leave the trim alone. So relax, it is easy to live with, at least until we get to the approach.

A little forethought given to the approach will go a long way. It is extremely handy to know the power settings that will give a 500 to 700 feet per minute descent in landing configuation. Generally, I fly approaches in the 120 knot to 140 knot speed range. Some experts suggest that a no-ASI approach should be flown with a power setting that gives the same 500 - 700 fpm descent at best rate of climb speed or V_{yse} for twins. This is unrealistic for some of the cleaner aerodynamic designs or ultra-high performance turbo-props and jets. For instance, achieving those speeds for landing may require an objectionable amount of flaps to be hanging out for a missed approach. The idea is to be at the proper speed to execute the missed approach by just adding power. It won't work if at the beginning of the approach all we did is reduce the power and throw the gear and flaps in the slip stream. A go-around is going to require a gear and flap retraction, and where is that going to leave us? It is going to leave us with a cruise trim setting and full power which results in some sort of a cruise-climb.

My recommendation is to fly the approach at a normal speed by just using normal power reductions and flopping out the gear and minimal amounts of flaps. Unless the approach speed of your aircraft is very near best rate of climb speed, there can be no advantage. In a no-ASI situation, a slower airspeed will be closer to the stall speed and raising the nose inadvertently while applying maximum power at the missed approach may cause us to complete the approach in an unorthodox manner. I don't think many pilots fly their approaches at V_y or V_{yse}; it is too slow for normal traffic flow. So, in an emergency, why go to the unfamiliar? Do it the same way *every* time regardless of the conditions.

When luck is going our way there will be an ILS at the destination. There's nothing like a glide slope for reassurance and the plane should just about flow through the approach in a normal manner. Once we break out of the clouds we can eyeball our attitude. From experience we should be able to land the plane without trouble. Should there be any doubt, though, keep the nose low until the aircraft is safely in ground effect.

In dealing with an ASI failure, a little trim will go a long way. We should endeavor to leave it alone as much as possible. For peace of mind we always have a back-up system, the stall warning. We all know what to do if we hear it—add power and release back pressure. Remember, power and the VSI will fill the gap during an ASI failure.

Another instrument that gets chosen for the examiner's sadistic enjoyment is the directional gyro. Most FAA check rides get the best of the DG. It really isn't the same magnitude of problem that the airspeed indicator failure can be. It is only hazardous when a pilot fails to notice it has departed. When it actually fails it will do one of two things. It will spin like a wheel or it will inconspicuously remain on the same heading, leading the pilot to believe that he really has it wired this flight.

In this condition we must look to the compass for adequate guidance. The jousting about of the compass card in rough air is a challenge to follow. The T & B comes in handy for direction changes. Making standard rate turns becomes the order of the day. To accurately turn the correct number of degrees, we must time them. This becomes an easy exercise if we divide the number of degrees of change that we need by three. For example, a change of 45 degrees would require a 15 second turn. It is the best policy not to begin timing until the needle or airplane wing (turn coordinator) touches the mark. I have found that turns come out closer to the money when I do this. As with all instrument failures, the face should be masked in order to minimize the chances for vertigo.

The one instrument that can fail and do the most harm is the altimeter. Its failure is usually due to a system failure of the pitot/static system, but occasionally a needle will stick. The failure of the ALT is a hard one to spot. There we are cruising along apparently holding altitude better than ever. Then we get cleared to a lower altitude. As we begin the descent there is no change in the needle's placement. What now? Well, we could begin timed descents if only we knew our altitude to start with.

The approach phase puts the pressure on. As a matter of fact, there aren't too many options except precision approach radar and these are few and far between. An encoding altimeter may offer some relief through ATC if its mechanism is not jammed as well. The only other good solution is to fly toward VFR conditions.

In an emergency, there is one other possible way to make it all work. The aircraft can be placed far enough out on the localizer that the glide slope can be intercepted and followed down. If we were at 6,000 feet, for example, and noticed right away that the ALT had failed, then if the altitude that we had was maintained until intercepting the localizer, we would be safe. Regardless of what they say about false glide slopes, a good experienced pilot should be able to tell the difference 90% of the time. The false glide slopes are generally erratic and would be hard to follow. The real glide slope is steady and can be followed with only slight riding of the elevators. I'm not saying it isn't important to intercept the glide slope at the proper altitude. It is important to have noticed the various idiosyncrasies in order to take advantage of them when an emergency crops up or an instrument craps out.

There is one other alternative to altimeter failure in aircraft equipped with altitude engines. Those are aircraft that have manifold pressure gauges. It should be considered a last resort, but the manifold pressure gauge may be used as an altimeter. To do this, the manifold pressure gauge reading must be converted to a usable quantity. A conversion factor of 950 is used to multiply each inch below standard pressure of 29.92. For example, if the MP gauge is showing 28.92, an inch lower in pressure than 29.92, then our altitude is 950 feet above mean sea level.

There are two glaring problems with using the manifold pressure gauge for an altimeter. If the engine is running it can't be used for anything but a power gauge. Also, if the pressure is other than standard, there is no Kollsman window to dial the correct pressure in.

To solve the first problem we don't have to shut the engine down to read the gauge. We can stick the heel of our shoe through the glass and render the instrument incapable of doing *anything*, but now we have no power indicator, so maybe the best thing to do is to wait until we can set the power for final approach and then give it a swift kick.

As far as the gauge not adjusting to pressure, don't sweat it. We couldn't read the dial for accuracy if we desired, it just isn't scaled for a use of this nature. We just do the best we can. If we're off five hundred feet at least we're in the ball park. Any other way we might have *no* indication of our altitude at all.

Most of these measures seem extreme and they are. Without a doubt the altimeter is the least dispensable instrument. If it should *ever* fail in your airplane and you are IFR it is time to declare an emergency. If a VFR area is nearby, this is the best alternative and then PAR is the next best choice. All these other possibilities should be left until the outcome of the flight seems due.

If there is one instrument on the panel that we can do without, it is the vertical speed indicator. To lose it is a nuisance and that's all. Oh, we may come out of our cruise altitude a little quicker than usual. But face it, the altimeter will fill in well when cross checked with the airspeed indicator. Only sloppy pilots need the VSI, so if it fails, "blow it off" and continue to the destination.

Failure of the turn and bank is also no special event. Flying in and out of large busy airports I seldom rely on it. Generally, all banks at my airline are 20 degrees and never more than 30 degrees with passengers aboard. We use the turn and bank as a check on our bank. We attempt not to exceed standard rate in most maneuvers whether we are on the gauges or in visual condition. At most of our speeds 20 degrees is less than standard rates. However, in a T & B failure, should it become necessary to make precise standard rate turns it can be quickly calculated by the formula:

$$\text{Bank angle} = \frac{\text{speed in knots}}{10} + 7$$

Thus an indicated speed of 120 knots requires a bank of 19 degrees to produce a standard rate turn of 3 degrees per second.

SYSTEM FAILURES

The vacuum/pressure system failure (Fig. 6-1) is the best known version of the partial panel. Without exception every instrument rating student should have battled his way over aircraft control when his instructor stuck his little soap holders on the faces of the affected instruments. The ADI and DG run off a vacuum pump in most light aircraft. When the needle of the suction gauge slowly nods over towards zero, the work begins. Although those two vacuum instruments are conveniences, all the necessities still remain that give pitch information, the ASI, VSI, and altimeter. There are two instruments for roll control: the turn and bank and compass. And last, but not least, the ball represents the yaw axis.

If your instrument ticket is new, you probably have an advantage on this situation. On the other hand, if a pilot has not practiced these emergency procedures in some time it will take a few minutes to organize a scan. Practice now and then on this type of partial panel and one should be adequately prepared. At the price of fuel these days, there is no reason to fly a special practice session; rather, practice these procedures on a real mission. It still wouldn't hurt to have an instrument rated pilot with you for a back up in case your simulated failure really buffaloes you.

Fig. 6-1. Vacuum/pressure system failure.

The one failure that a pilot can usually have control over is the pitot/static system failure (Fig. 6-2). When this system fails it is usually due to blockage of the pitot tube or static port by either insects or an accretion of ice. In many planes there are two controls, pitot heat and an alternate static source valve. Using one of these or both we can normally expect the failure to be temporary.

The instruments that are affected by a pitot/static failure are the airspeed indicator, altimeter and VSI. If there is no alternate static source on the plane a sharp blow to the face of one of the instruments will serve as an alternate source. Although any of the affected instruments will serve this purpose it might make a difference in which one we choose. Most pilots would probably choose the VSI as the point of attack, thinking that this is the least valuable instrument. There may be some ramifications in choosing this instrument that may make you wish you had not. When the VSI glass is shattered, the static air to the other instruments now must flow through the capillary tube. The size of this tube means that flow will be slow which will create an aggravating lag in the airspeed indicator and altimeter. Also, the VSI will now read backward. This peculiarity may suggest that another instrument might be a better choice. The altimeter or airspeed would cause the system to function more normally. My choice would be the ASI, as any inadvertent damage to this particular instrument would be easier to live with as we discussed under individual instrument failure.

A few pitot/static system failures are beyond the ability of the pilot to correct from within the cockpit. For example, a mechanic could have accidentally connected the pitot air to the static system, resulting in the immediate and unfortunate failure of the altimeter and VSI at takeoff. The airspeed would continue to work, but in an unusual manner. The final result is a touchy situation.

The first rule in any emergency is not to do anything very soon after it has been noted. The best thing to do is to take inventory of just what has been affected and what we have left. In this case, we should note our time and estimate how fast we are climbing by experience in the type of aircraft. That will be our only knowledge or estimate of our height above the ground. Another couple of things we could note is the tachometer and manifold pressure. They both fall off at a fixed rate. The tachometer may be hard to use unless a pilot is extraordinarily familiar with it. The manifold pressure is a better measure as it drops off an inch for every one

Fig. 6-2. Pitot/static system failure.

thousand feet of climb. For those airplanes having automatic wastegates on turbo-charged engines there is precious little that can be done to estimate altitude. There is one shot in the dark and that's just what it is. The pilot of a turbo-charged automatic wastegate aircraft could note the temperature and apply the standard lapse rate. Usually, when flying in cloud, the lapse rate does not hold as the atmosphere is layered by temperature inversions.

All these alternatives may be little comfort in a pressure cooker cockpit. It could be our only help unless we have PAR near by. The best thing to do is concentrate on manifold pressure and the attitude indicator for altitude and speed control.

The electrical system hurts very little on the flight panel. The turn and bank or turn coordinator is the only instrument that will go on the fritz (Fig. 6-3). Of course, a great many other things will be giving trouble like radios and lights. It may become impossible to see the other instruments that are working. Surely it's obvious, but we should check the generator(s) circuit breaker and reset it. Also, the turn and bank has a circuit breaker. If the lights aren't failing then check that one, too.

Now, we come to the discussion of multiple system failures. I always say, "they like to kick you while you're down." With Murphy's Law at full tilt boogie, don't worry; *nothing* is going to turn out all right.

One combination, the vacuum-electrical system failure (Fig.

Fig. 6-3. Electrical system failure.

6-4): This is the simplest of failures to handle because it is the only multi-system failure that does not take the altimeter away from us. In this failure we will lose the ADI, DG and turn and bank. The challenge of making turns with only the magnetic compass becomes real. There is no way to make this task easy. The best idea is to make small banks according to feel or kinesthesia. We all know that kinesthesia is unreliable and that is why all these instruments were invented in the first place. Yet it is possible to tell roughly how large our bank is by controlling our control input. This vague information will have to be our guide. As long as we can rely on the altimeter, our banks be they shallow or steep should not become dangerous.

Whenever the pitot/static and electrical system go out together we lose four instruments, one of which is the altimeter (Fig. 6-5). The failure can be handled without much of a problem because two of our favorite instruments are left, the ADI and DG. Bank angles and maintaining headings are easy. Climbs and descents can be made by using time as we discussed with an earlier failure type. Climbs may be a tad more difficult than the descents because positioning a pitch up attitude by use of the ADI does not always yield the same rate of climb. Climbs, as we know, will vary with altitude. The descents can usually be estimated to be the same.

Using the ADI to establish 500 feet per minute descents is an old trick. It works particularly well in airplanes equipped with constant speed propellers. Basically, it works this way. The wings of the airplane are lowered beneath the horizon. The top of the wings should abutt with the bottom of the horizon line. Power in constant speed prop aircraft does not even need to be reduced, except every thousand feet. This will help to keep track of the altitude as well as allow a normal descent. As we mentioned earlier, normality lends a needed dimension to emergency. With planes that have fixed pitch props a decrease of about 400 - 500 rpm will allow a 500 feet per minute descent. It would help tremendously in a multiple failure such as this one to know the exact power setting required.

Probably, the worst of all combinations of multi-system failures is the vacuum- pitot/static failure (Fig. 6-6). We are left with extremely little in positive information. We have no indications of pitch attitude other than power and trim, and of course the venerable stall warning. For roll are the turn and bank and the compass for direction.

Airspeed in this type of failure is a main concern. We are outright relegated to the speed at which we were trimmed when the failure occurred. At least we have a knowledge of our speed.

As we just discussed, speed may be controlled by power. Descents may be initiated by reducing power at a rate of one inch of manifold pressure per 100 feet of descent *or* about 100 rpm in fixed pitch prop aircraft. The techniques are a combination of our individual instrument failures of airspeed and altimeter, fundamen-

Fig. 6-4. Vacuum-electrical system failure.

tally. There isn't much to work with, but a little common sense will go far in making the flight a success.

It could be any flight at night, the nightmare they said that would be so unlikely, a million to one. But it happens. An electrical fire begins as a smoldering and then bursts into flame. As you reach for the fire extinguisher the flames frolic about the wiring and pitot/static lines. Quickly the flames are extinguished but the insides of the panel have been melted and fused into a charred mess. With flames snuffed, it becomes apparent that we're flying at night with no power and no instruments. It's the worst—total system failure. The rest is up to the Lord, right? *Wrong.*

Get out your flashlight to begin with. A quick inventory will reveal only the ball and the magnetic compass in working order. The best thing to do is to head for a VFR area. If that is out of reach, head for an area that offers the flattest terrain where a descent would be least hazardous. If all directions look equally hopeless, head south. The compass needle is more sensitive to southerly headings. Straight and level and shallow turns should be easiest, but not easy.

Next, we should make a gradual reduction in power. I would suggest not too much. The goal here is to set up a minimum sink rate; 100 to 200 feet per minute is perfect. Of course, we won't know our sink rate. Experts say that a 100-foot per minute sink rate is good for landing floatplanes on a glassy surface; by the same token it would be good to help maintain control in our awkward

Fig. 6-5. Pitot/static—electrical system failure.

Fig. 6-6. Vacuum—pitot/static system failure.

situation. Whenever we break out of the clouds we will be under control and able to find a suitable landing area.

With all the things that can go wrong, we could worry ourselves sick. If one tends to occupy his mind with the results of such failures, may I suggest a fool-proof alternative.

I refer you to the nearest pet store. Get yourself a cat and a duck.

Chapter 7
Upgrading to High Performance Avionics

The early to middle 1960's brought about the birth of an electronic marvel—the integrated circuit. We are most familiar with its use in electronic pocket calculators and televisions.

The significance of this development to aviation was the reduction in the size of components and of course, weight. Since about 1968, the complexity of the cockpit has gradually increased, until today many single-engine aircraft are as well equipped as the airliners (Fig. 7-1). This has had a two-sided effect on flying. On the positive side it has increased the utility of the general aviation fleet to a point that was not thought feasible or safe just 15 years ago. The *negative* side of the coin is that many pilots have dropped out, thinking that the equipment is too complicated or that flying is no longer fun anymore with all these electronics. In this writer's opinion, nothing could be farther from the truth. Although I fly for a scheduled airline my knowledge largely came from reading magazines and books such as this one.

The electronics in the cockpit not only help us finish more flights, they can even be fun to use in their own right. So, in the following pages, we will introduce and explain in simple terms what these new electronic navigation devices do and how to use them. The photos on these pages are courtesy of Rockwell International, Collins Division. They have worked with me on this project and provided a great deal of help. I choose Collins Avionics because I fly with them every day and feel qualified to explain how they work.

Fig. 7-1. Moving up to high performance avionics is the dream of every instrument pilot. This airliner is outfitted like a dream come true.

THE INITIAL UPGRADE

When a pilot moves up into higher performance aircraft, such as from a Cessna 182 to a light twin of the Cessna 400 series, the move usually involves more than larger engines and complex hydraulic systems. The first thing a pilot notices when he sticks his head through the cockpit door is that there's a lot of "stuff" up there (Fig. 7-2). Next, he must realistically ask himself, do I know how to use it? If he doesn't, he might need a little dual on those avionics. Then again, if the pilot is progressive and reads a great deal (such as TAB Book 2301, *Upgrading Your Airplane's Avionics*) he may be hours ahead of the game.

The most common move up is to a flight director system. In lightplanes these are usually two 4-inch instruments (Fig. 7-3). They take the place of the artificial horizon and directional gyro. The top instrument of the two is called an attitude director indicator (ADI). The bottom instrument is known as an HSI or horizontal situation indicator.

The ADI is probably the biggest mystery to pilots who have not used one. Essentially, the instrument is flown as an artificial horizon (Fig. 7-4). There is an attitude tape that depicts earth and sky relative to an airplane symbol, so there is nothing different there. There are marks at the top of the instrument which depict the various angles of bank such as straight and level, 10, 20, 30, and

Fig. 7-2. There's a lot of stuff up there. But think of the fun (courtesy Cessna).

60 degrees. So far it's all the same. The difference or complexity comes when we realize that the ADI also incorporates the VOR and ILS navigation instruments, instead of the cross-hairs that many of us cut our instrument teeth on.

On the left side of the ADI, we find the glide slope pointer and its accompanying dots or scale. Below the center airplane display and above the inclinometer we find the localizer pointer. In the upper right hand corner is a light that illuminates at decision height and below that is a radio altimeter scale from zero to 200 feet.

A pilot who is unaccustomed to looking at an ADI (such as the one depicted in Fig. 7-5) must wonder if the old cross-hairs idea wasn't simpler and easier to understand, not to mention better placed. Well, all those little pointers are what we call the raw data. And, although the plane can be flown well down the ILS with it, that is not the way that it is done. In the photo, notice that the airplane symbol is a triangle or delta. The symbolic airplane remains stationary. However, above it are a set of bars that move. These are called *command bars*. The command bars are controlled by a flight guidance computer which position them in the proper place to intercept a given localizer and glide slope. The idea is that by control pressures, we move the symbolic airplane into the nitch of the command bars regardless of where they are. By keeping the symbol airplane flush against the bottom of the command bars, interception and capturing of both localizer and glide slope is done perfectly and smoothly—in fact, much better than the best pilot could do using cross-hairs or raw data.

One other point—the inclinometer on this instrument makes monitoring all three axes of flight incredibly easy. They are all

Fig. 7-3. Usually, the first upgrade in avionics is to a flight director system. This is the FDS-84 system by Collins using two 4-inch instruments (courtesy Collins Avionics).

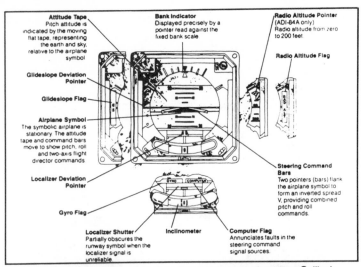

Attitude Tape
Pitch attitude is indicated by the moving flat tape, representing the earth and sky, relative to the airplane symbol

Glideslope Deviation Pointer

Glideslope Flag

Airplane Symbol
The symbolic airplane is stationary. The attitude tape and command bars move to show pitch, roll and two-axis flight director commands

Localizer Deviation Pointer

Gyro Flag

Bank Indicator
Displayed precisely by a pointer read against the fixed bank scale

Radio Altitude Pointer
(ADI-84A only)
Radio altitude from zero to 200 feet

Radio Altitude Flag

Steering Command Bars
Two pointers (bars) flank the airplane symbol to form an inverted spread V, providing combined pitch and roll commands.

Localizer Shutter
Partially obscures the runway symbol when the localizer signal is unreliable.

Inclinometer

Computer Flag
Annunciates faults in the steering command signal sources.

Fig. 7-4. The FDS-84 ADI broken down into components (courtesy Collins).

Fig. 7-5. A close-up of an ADI in action. Shown is the Collins FDS85 flight director system—V-Bar attitude indicator with digital radio altitude and decision height annunciator (courtesy Collins).

there on one instrument. This should be a feature on all artificial horizons, whether they are part of a flight director system or not.

Let's now turn our attention to the HSI. Some aircraft without a complete flight director system incorporate this tool into the flight panel. You won't find a flight director system without one, however. I think of an HSI as a map plan view. In other words, the

Fig. 7-6. Collins FDS-85 flight director system—Horizontal situation indicator has full time distance display, time-shared groundspeed time-to-station/ elapsed time window, VNAV display capability, and remote HCP-85 heading/ course panel (courtesy Collins).

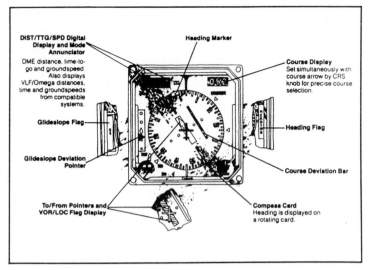

DIST/TTG/SPD Digital Display and Mode Annunciator
DME distance, time-to-go and groundspeed Also displays VLF/Omega distances, time and groundspeeds from compatible systems.

Glideslope Flag

Glideslope Deviation Pointer

To/From Pointers and VOR/LOC Flag Display

Heading Marker

Course Display
Set simultaneously with course arrow by CRS knob for precise course selection.

Heading Flag

Course Deviation Bar

Compass Card
Heading is displayed on a rotating card.

Fig. 7-7. The FDS-84 HSI broken down into components for familiarization (courtesy Collins).

instrument depicts the position of our aircraft as it would look if it were superimposed on an enroute chart.

The HSI in Fig. 7-6 has a DME display in the upper corner as well as glide slope information on the left side. Thus, this instrument can be used for flying VOR or ILS approaches by itself. We must use raw data, however. To use the HSI, we should think of it as a replacement for the cross-hair or needle VOR head arrangement. Where with the traditional VOR head we had an OBS setting, this is replaced by a course setting on the HSI. They are one and the same. The difference is in how they are depicted (Fig. 7-7). For example, the OBS setting or course setting in the photo is 015 degrees. The course deviation indicator is off the left. Hence, we must correct to the left to intercept the radial and place us squarely on course. The airplane in the center of the display shows the aircraft doing just that. Simply, the deviation bar and the course arrow rotate with the compass card for continuous, natural depiction of position in reference to the selected course. The digital course selection display in the upper right hand corner makes precise course adjustments more convenient.

The selector in the lower left corner of the HSI is to move the heading "bug" and select which DME function that is desired. DIST stands for distance to or from the station, TTG is for time to go and SPD is groundspeed in knots.

Fig. 7-8. The new Collins ADS-80 air data system consists of (left to right): the ADC-80F central air data computer; TAI-80 true airspeed/temp indicator; ALI-80 encoding altimeter; PRE-80 altitude preselector/alerter; and the VSI-80 vertical speed indicator (courtesy Collins).

113

Fig. 7-9. VSI-80 vertical speed indicator (courtesy Collins).

If there are any questions in your mind about how these function, take a trip out to the airport. Many time, there are corporate pilots there waiting for their bosses to return who would welcome the distraction from doing nothing to take time and show you their operation. If you are lucky you'll get to go aboard one of the bizjets and check their equipment out. Incidentally, they usually use the 5-inch models of flight director systems pictured here. These have added options and advantages.

AIR DATA SYSTEMS

A pilot moving into bizjets may have to deal with many new devices. Adjusting to the speed that the aircraft flies may not be the only problem in transitioning to a high performance airplane. In most jets, there is a battery of flight instruments that are interdependent (Figs. 7-8 through 7-10). These instruments are coordinated, so to speak, through a central air data computer. This computer does things like measure outside air temperature, correct it for ram rise, and convert indicated airspeed to true airspeed. Once these things are done the computer easily converts the airspeed into a Mach number. The speed of sound is directly dependant on temperature, hence the need of a computer to reduce pilot work load. Many flight plans are fulfilled by maintaining an accurate Mach speed. As fuel is burned, the power on a turbine engine must be reduced for the aircraft will be lighter and will travel faster. The idea is to keep fuel burn to a minimum and operational costs per mile down. The air data system lets the crew do this without constantly recomputing Mach numbers and standard temperatures.

Other safety and pilot workload reduction features are incorporated into an airdata system. According to Collins engineers, the air data instruments actually track the autopilot since

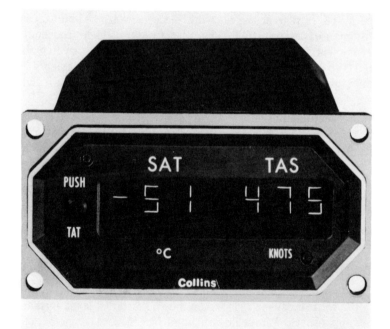

Fig. 7-10. Part of the air data system—TAI-80 true airspeed/temperature indicator. Static air temperature is normally displayed, along with a digital readout of TAS. Total air temperature is displayed with the button on the left of the indicator is pushed (courtesy Collins).

the autopilot and instruments are fed from the same pressure sensing sources. Even though the instruments use the same pressure sources, altitude and airspeed channels and computations are independent which reduces the risk that a single failure would totally disable the system.

Air data systems are a way of life above FL 250, and who's to say that you won't come in contact with one sooner or later? At least now you are familiar with their purpose. Using them is straightforward—just read the dials.

HIGH FREQUENCY EQUIPMENT

When long distance travel over water is required of an aircraft, then high frequency radio equipment is required and necessary. The VHF equipment such as VOR's and the communication frequencies that we are familiar with are line of sight signals only. This means the curvature of the earth will as some point and altitude intercede between an airplane and a given station. The station can no longer be received. This means that contact with such VHF stations across the world's oceans would be impractical to initiate or maintain. Thus, the need for high frequency equipment for communications. A high frequency wavelength tends to conform to the curvature of the earth and is usable for a much greater distance. This is why transoceanic aircraft use it and very low frequencies (VLF) for navigation.

These units also have an upper sideband mode which produces a narrow modulation width of any given signal and thus will carry farther or can be received at a greater range. Many CB's and amateur radio rigs have this feature and you may already be acquainted with it. Also, one of the features of the Collins (Fig. 7-11) equipment is its ability to program 16 channels for radio-telephone work. That will keep the boys in the back busy taking care of business and out of the cockpit trying to interfere with yours.

THE LATEST: RADAR NAVIGATION

It has been a long time coming. Pilots must have wished for it in the earliest days of radar when they noticed that some terrain features such as a lake could be painted. The modern technology of integrated circuits has reduced size and weight of electronic packages to where many things are possible and the development of radar navigation systems for light aircraft is perhaps the ultimate.

Fig. 7-11. The full array of available high performance avionics. Most of these are used in rack-mounted installation (courtesy Collins).

Here's what the RNS-300 navigation system by Collins does. It makes it possible to plot course lines to OMEGA/VLF waypoints, RNAV waypoints, VORTACs, or intersections defined by a heading line and course line. It also has a page data mode with a non-volatile memory (will not forget when shut down) which maintains 17 pages of performance tables, procedures checklists, and any other pilot—generated information for recall. A real nice function is that of an emergency page that can be recalled instantly.

Let's explore this latest state-of-the-art in aircraft navigation. This marvel called the RNS-300 interprets and displays raw navigation data from a primary VOR/DME, RNAV or VLF/OMEGA systems. Then the aircraft's position and progress is computed to create an "in motion" picture with stations, waypoints, course lines and heading lines on the radar screen which is now a CRT display as well.

By using the nav receivers, the waypoints or stations can be moved anywhere on the display on any range scale. Even when the points are off scale or behind the aircraft, "selectable course lines" will indicate the planned flight route. In this way it is easy to stay oriented to nav stations and ATC directives.

The display moves in accordance with real time, so it is constantly updated. On approach to airports it adequately displays

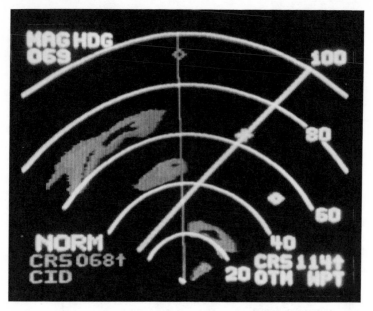

Fig. 7-12. This is the RNS-300 radar navigation screen. Note the course line from top to bottom and the wider, more prominent RNAV course line with a waypoint (courtesy Collins).

the aircraft's position to fixes and the runway. The great thing is that vectors can be anticipated and double-checked against ATC. How many times have you gotten a bad turn to final?

The RNS-300 color codes everything. Although the photos here are black and white, the left side is generally in yellow and the right side is magenta. Three-letter identifiers are shown for each data block at the bottom corners unless it is a waypoint and then it is designated (WPT). In addition, each color code works off of an independent HSI. The yellow data is from the left HSI or Captain's side. The magenta data is from the copilot's side. Also, in the data blocks you will notice an arrow. This arrow points to indicate the position of the station, whether it is ahead or behind the airplane.

One of the most significant features is that the radar and pictorial navigation system can work at the same time. The active HSI will designate a white heading line to map alternate course around thunderstorm activity. In addition, this function can also be used for displaying ATC vectors.

Now, let's examine some sample situations on how to use this marvel. In Fig. 7-12, notice the two data blocks. The one labeled NORM is yellow in color and is represented by the course line that runs straight up and down and has the diamond between the 80 and 100-mile radar range rings. The heavier course line is an RNAV course line from the OTM VORTAC and is magenta in color. It corresponds with the lower right and data block.

There is also a white magnetic heading line of 069 degrees that parallels the yellow line.

If this was our weather situation we would want to shoot the gap between the line of cells. The largest gap is about 20 miles wide between the 20 and 40 mile range rings. By plotting a course as in this photo we can navigate accurately between cells. First, we would want to fly the 068 degree course (yellow) line until intercepting the RNAV course line. Then we would turn to 114 degrees and track that RNAV course to avoid the storm cells to best advantage.

Here's another way to avoid the weather. In Fig. 7-13 the aircraft heading is 098 degrees with the course to the CID VORTAC to the left on a 062 degree bearing. The HSI heading "bug" is turned to a heading that will avoid weather to the left of the present magnetic heading shown in the photo. There is bearing readout to the OTM VORTAC in the lower right (magenta) data

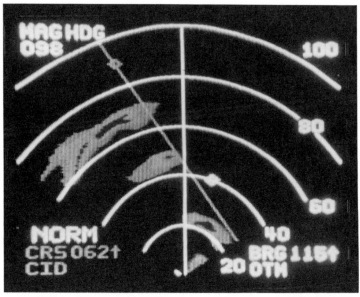

Fig. 7-13. The idea here is to circumnavigate the weather; when the pilot deems it all clear of weather, then the flight to the OTM VORTAC can be resumed by activating course 2 (CRS 2).

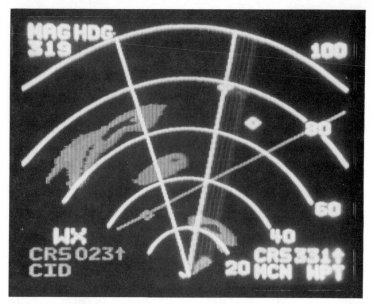

Fig. 7-14. This method uses both HSI controlled course lines and a white heading line directed by the active HSI.

box. The VORTAC is depicted on the display at the lower right center of the photo as a diamond. These functions are displayed because the pilot activated his NAV 2 on the data control panel.

The idea is to circumnavigate the weather; when the pilot deems it all clear, then the flight to the OTM VORTAC can be resumed by activating course 2 (CRS 2). Then, a course line would appear on the display and the plane could navigate by radio direct to the VORTAC.

Here's my favorite method for using the Radar Navigation System for avoiding weather. This one really fits since we ordinarily fly headings around weather. This method uses both HSI controlled course lines and a white heading line directed by the active HSI. In Fig. 7-14 the magnetic heading is 319 degrees. That heading line runs from the radar focal point to the 11 o'clock position. As you can see, this line is well clear of weather through the 30-mile range on the radar. At that point it intercepts the yellow course line of 023 degrees from the CID VORTAC. The CID VORTAC is depicted by the diamond. Ideally, we should now fly the 023 degree radial to clear the weather at 40 miles, and then resume our flight planned route of 331 degrees to the MCN waypoint. The waypoint is represented by the star and MCN

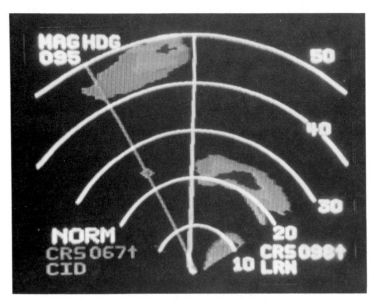

Fig. 7-15. The RNS-300 using VLF/OMEGA for navigation display.

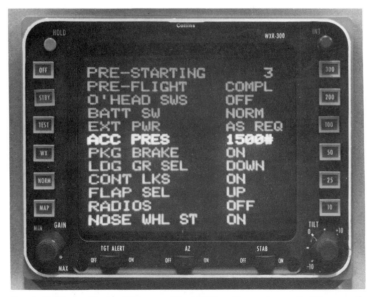

Fig. 7-16. Electronic checklists are with us! This unit can store up to 17 pages of important data including an emergency page.

Fig. 7-17. Notice the "T" in the upper right hand corner that tells us we are painting weather.

VORTAC is represented at the 70-mile range right of center. Now, *that* is what I call accurate weather avoidance! Naturally, the weather will be moving, but we can easily replot courses in seconds to adjust to the situation.

Speaking of high performance avionics, the radar navigation system is compatible with LORAN, VLF/OMEGA. In Fig. 7-15, the magenta line is tuned to a VLF waypoint beyond the radar range indicated. After tuning in the VLF waypoint and course line the other options that we discussed in the previous photographs are available to be used in order to avoid weather.

Electronic checklists are with us. The radar navigation system developed by Collins incorporates up to 17 pages of checklists and performance charts. As with the entire unit the checklists are color coded. In Fig. 7-16, the brightly accented line which reads "ACC PRES" is in blue. The items above it are in green indicating that they have been done. Below that line the lines are in yellow which indicate they have not been done. The pilots can move the blue line ahead or backwards by the control panel underneath the CRT display as shown in the photo. The arrows indicate which way the "line of use" will move. Each line in use will then automatically be colored blue.

One other great feature is that of target alert. Notice the "T" in the upper right corner of the display in Fig. 7-17. Whenever page data or nav only mode is being viewed, the "T" will flash on and off if contourable weather is approaching. Then the pilot can switch to a radar mode and check the situation.

Not shown in any of these photographs is a remote hand-held unit for programming the page data section. It is about the size of a pocket calculator and has letters of the alphabet and numbers for quantitative entries. Thus, any page can be changed at any time, even in flight.

The age of avionics in the cockpit is here to stay. We're not equipped like the Battlestar Galactica or Captain Kirk's Enterprise yet, but we're well down the road toward that type of machine and environment. With restricted airspace growing more each year (at least that which requires more onboard avionics to enter), the pilot of today and tomorrow needs to learn to deal with it. It may be expensive, but it also may be more fun.

Chapter 8
Quick Tips

Perhaps you've noticed that there is a great deal of information crammed on every approach plate. Some of this is landing information, some is takeoff information. Some is a plan view of the airport. *Most* of that information is *clutter* when we should be concentrating on the approach at hand.

Several times, I have been well into approach control airspace and told to expect a parallel ILS to runway 17R, for instance. By the vectors that the controller is issuing us, I can tell that we are just prior to turning final for that ILS approach. The radios have been tuned, identified, and all briefings and checklists are complete. The crew's train of thought is concentrated on completing the approach and missed approach procedures. Then the controller throws a wrench into the whole works. We are informed to now change our approach to runway 17L.

The crew goes into immediate action. The only reason the cockpit isn't filled with pandemonium, flying approach books and ripped out radios is because of experience. The key to that experience can be any pilot's, regardless of the number of hours in his logbooks. A pilot who has flown a great many hours knows just what to look for in order to simplify learning the approach. Of course, all information on the approach plate is important at some time, but when a pilot is pinched for time most of the plate can be disregarded.

Fundamentally, there are only five items that must be learned or done before approach is commenced. The missed approach procedure must be learned or done before an approach is commenced. The missed approach procedure must be committed to memory. Usually, I only endeavor to remember the initial altitude to climb and whether that altitude is followed by a right or left turn or straight out. Occasionally, the climb requires a turn at the same time. The copilot is instructed in case of a missed approach that he will quickly brief on any further turns or altitudes and then reset the radios for the fix we are to fly to. Possibly this won't work in a single pilot operation or in mountainous terrain, so adapt it to the situation.

The second of the five items that needs to be done is to tune and identify localizers, VORs, DMEs, test marker beacons and set locator beacons. As we do this we should double check our frequencies because many times localizer and VOR frequencies will be printed very near each other and it is easy to confuse them.

Thirdly, we should notice the time to missed approach. At this point we should ask for a wind check if one is available or use the one from the ATIS. Remember, the time is predicated on groundspeed, *not* approach airspeed. However, I've found with most headwinds there isn't much difference in time because the winds change all the way down the approach. Tailwinds will foul us up something terrific.

Fourth, we should set our OBS or course pointer on an HSI to the heading for the final approach. We should memorize the heading, and at least study any headings that may be involved in a procedure turn.

Last, but not least, we should commit to memory all necessary altitudes for the approach. These may include altitudes of intermediate approach fixes. For example, the approach to DFW Regional has a fix at 10 DME. Unless otherwise instructed by ATC, all aircraft are to cross at or above 3,000 feet. The glide slope can be intercepted at that point and followed to the runway. Of course, we don't want to forget the altitude of the final approach fix or our DH or MDA.

All that took quite a few words to say. So, many of you are sitting there wondering how is all this easy to remember in a clutch situation. "That guy has been flying for years and he expects *me* to grasp it in a minute?". Well, that's just what you can do. For the next few minutes, sit in your easy chair and commit this acronym and its meaning to memory. You'll never have a problem reacting to changed approaches or those sprung on you late in the game when you should have been told miles ago. The word is MARTHA. And here's how they stand:

*M*issed
*A*pproach
*R*adios
*T*imes
*H*eading
*A*ltitudes

Simple? Right! Just remember that each letter applies to the approach situation. Students have trouble remembering what altitude means. I usually say to myself when I'm briefing the approach that the "altitudes are 2300 over the marker down to 1289 for DH." It is a handy item and will make a professional out of you in a hurry.

KEEPING THE NEEDLES IN LINE

After all the flight instruction instrument students receive, there still remains some room for improvement. Mainly, this is due to most instrument students being taught to be *mechanical* about their approach to flying approaches instead of being *analytical*. For example, I was taught to control my wanderings on the glide slope with power. That can make the ride appear to passengers like you aren't sure what you're supposed to be doing. In essence, you don't and I didn't. Power is only used for setting the approach speed and for non-precision approaches and to set the rate of sink.

How do we fly an approach with finesse? Well, a great many factors go into it. Like we've said throughout the book, doing things routinely has a calming effect on everyone involved. Hence, we should always throw the gear at the outer marker and make the final power adjustment as the glide slope comes into center scale. Then the glide slope can be followed easily by elevator pressure.

Most students and newly rated instrument pilots have not developed what almost is a sixth sense about the glide slope. If you ever have the chance, watch a *professional* fly an ILS—and I don't mean an instructor. He'll seem to make corrections almost before anything has gone astray. There are two reasons for this. His concentration is more atuned to what he is doing and must do. Moreover, he is closely watching for any needle fluctuation. What I've told my students in the past is to watch the needles ever so carefully, so that if they move even one-sixteenth of an inch, begin a correction immediately. Beginning a correction early means the correction will be small and passengers probably won't even notice.

On non-precision approaches there is one technique that bothers me and it bothers passengers. We all learned early that it is important to descend to the minimum descent altitude as rapidly as possible. Unfortunately, we may have to sacrifice an average rate of sink, say 500 fpm, to complete the approach. However, there is no reason to put the nose down in an attitude where everyone is hanging from their safety belt. Certainly, fat Aunt Clara is not going to dig it.

The way to control sink is with power and *not* elevator in this instance. Of course, if the airspeed becomes too low we may be able to increase power and lower the nose a little more and recover our necessary rate of sink. Doing this would not be uncomfortable to our riders, but might necessitate an adjustment in our time to missed approach.

Another little-discussed item, and possibly so because it is often intangible, is the wind correction angle on any approach. While this rule is far from being set in concrete, it does give a good pilot something to shoot for. In fact, it may be one of those things that makes the difference between a good pilot and a great pilot.

Have you ever thought about how the wind changes with altitude? It more often than not swings around to the right or clockwise the higher we go. For example, the wind at 3,000 feet may be 240 degrees at 10 knots and 250 degrees at 12 knots in the neighborhood of 6,000 feet. The reason for this is skin friction—skin friction from the surface of the earth because it is turning west to east and thus deflects the wind somewhat to the left in the northern hemisphere and to be right in the southern half of the world. This has some effect on the wind right down to the surface. Thus, as we lose altitude in our planes the wind will move to the left. Apply this to our instrument approaches, we should soon realize that as we descend down the localizer or what have you, we should be taking a little more of the right correction out. If the initial correction was to the left, then we will find ourselves adding more left correction as we descend. As I said at the outset, this is not a rule without a great many exceptions, yet you'll find that it holds true a great deal. This rule falls apart in areas near thunderstorms or fronts because local windshears are making the flying rules then.

A few words on flying windshears during approaches—they can be dangerous, as we all know. The FAA has installed windshear detection equipment at most air carrier airports. It consists of several wind direction sensors placed around the field.

When windshears are probable, the tower will issue wind checks something like this.

"Cessna 19Q, center field wind is 160 at 15 knots, west field boundary 280 at 22 gusting 28."

That gives a good indication that a front, or sometimes a thunderstorm, is very near or on the airport. Naturally, we'd *see* the T-storm, but fronts may be invisible. From our windcheck we could expect our headwind to shift to somewhat of a tailwind if we were on approach to a southerly runway like 16 or 18. In a situation like this, we could expect a big bump and our airspeed to increase. Out of the two possible wind shear situations (an increase in airspeed or a decrease), this is the easiest to cope with. In marginal conditions, though, and down close to the runway an airspeed increase could cause a marked tendency to float and force the pilot to make a rash decision to go-around. The answer is to be ready, and don't force the plane onto the runway. Wait a moment or else you'll have to shoot the approach again.

If the opposite type of windshear is noted, then we can expect our airspeed to fall off markedly and a high rate of sink to follow. If we are armed with this information ahead of time we can carry extra airspeed on approach. This will counteract the tendency to sink very much and give us a margin of safety.

TRY IT ONE MORE TIME OR SPLIT?

The Cessna 402 was cleared for the approach. The pilot's skillful hand guided the aircraft down the VOR radial toward the airport. Descending quickly to the MDA, the pilot divided his attention to locate the airport visually. The seconds were ticking away and the missed approach point was near. Just then, a hole opened and he caught a glimpse of the runway lights. The plane was at MDA, a good 350 feet above the runway and already past the threshold.

The decision here is a common one in aviation. Almost every day, somewhere, some pilot must make the decision to shoot the approach again or go on the alternate.

If you were faced with this decision what would you do? It probably depends on two factors: fuel and weather. First, when the runway was sighted did the clouds extend well below the airplane? If so, how large was the hole? If the hole was not much larger than the airplane it probably won't do any good to go back around. Remember, minimums don't change, only the clouds can change (Fig. 8-1).

Fig. 8-1. Missed approach? Heck, we can't even get off the ground!

Fuel plays an awfully large part in the decision. Another approach will eat up another ten minutes'worth of fuel. Can you afford that? Did you plan to have extra fuel? Another thing one needs to know before jumping off is what the weather is doing at the alternate. If it has deteriorated, multiple approaches or a hold might be what is in store before touching ground again. Where many pilots have gone wrong in the past is on this point. Multiple approaches at the destination, brought on by get-home-itis, has caused them to run well into their 45 minute reserve. The result is a nail biting, hair splitting photo finish at the alternate.

A compromise that I have used and that has served to keep my flying career without incident is to check for the closest alternate to my destination. I try to do this during the preflight briefing, but sometimes weather does not allow the closest alternate. Sometimes, though, the closest alternate has improved by the time I miss approach at my destination. Upon missing the approach, I immediately request the controller to obtain weather for the closest alternate, calling it by name. If the weather is acceptable I divert to there, saving myself fuel, time and anxiety.

After reaching that alternate, I again check weather at the original destination. If it has improved then we load up with fuel and go try it again, knowing I can return safely to the alternate. Sure, this is an inconvenience, but ordinarily one never starts wishing he was on the ground when he has no fuel to go anywhere. My rule is if the approach is missed, then I'll catch it next time I fly in. Not this time. The only exception I can think of is when the approach was flown poorly and the miss was due to that.

A PLAN FOR THE INEXPERIENCED

Becoming a competent instrument pilot can be a tremendously satisfying experience. No other phase of aviation offers the wide range of experiences that filing IFR does. It is a great experience completing a flight just as the pros do it. Falling into line behind one of TWA's red and white three-holers in anticipation of punching the clouds right behind him swells the emotion in most pilots. In fact, its just damned hard *not* to let it show all over your face. Getting a directive from approach control to follow one of those sporty little DC-9s puts a guy's ego right up there with the rest of the world's important people. He is intimately involved in the magic of flying in clouds and the number of people who can do that is relatively few.

Indeed, it does seem mystical at times. Then, there are the times when decisions count, and paths through thunderstorm alley are carved precariously close to your own and the plane's limits. The learning experience is as much a part of living and the desire to live as any faced by man. Yet, each successful flight usually means the pilot is more adequately prepared to go out and fly the next one more safely with a greater chance of completion. The process known simply as experience becomes what has been and what will be.

The road to experience can be strewn with objects that at times seem to threaten a pilot's very existence. But a pilot has the control over his destiny at all times. Even the most foolish decisions to push ahead when one should have turned back can be coped with if good logic and operation procedures are followed from that point onward. The reality is that beginning to fly actual instrument conditions on our own can be a frightful experience, even when dangerous factors don't exist. I was extremely nervous the first time I flew actual instruments and remember it to this day.

Early in the morning the clouds were building into mega-proportions. They had that big white cauliflower look. Oh, they probably weren't as huge as I imagined them, but they looked tough to a neophyte like me. I summoned an instructor friend of mine, and asked if he thought they'd be rough.

"Oh, I reckon so. They'll be bumpy all right, but they can be handled," he added.

"Well, would you fly through 'em?"

"Sure, it's not like they're thunderstorms or something." He seemed sure of himself.

Well, at this point I had no idea that I'd be flying a single-engine VFR charter to Houston that day, but fly somebody over there I did. Preparing for the return I checked the weather; it was pretty good. Still, there were all those towering cumulus hunkering around up there. Finally, I decided to get my feet wet. I filed IFR and asked for 6,000, figuring that ought to put me right in the belly of those devils.

Sure enough, climbing eastbound I punched into my first one, gritting my teeth all the way. Sneaking a peek, I noticed the wings were still out there. By golly, old E.J. was right! I *can* fly through these dudes.

I began to get a little confidence. Far from cocky, but I was sure 8,000 feet would be more fun. It got me up out of the crud and splitting the sunlight between those giant pillars of white. The feeling was ecstatic. There I was in my own little fun house in the sky. That thunderstorm over at my nine o'clock position was causing a lot of chatter on the frequency, but I wasn't saying anything. I was just grinnin'.

It takes a lot of guts, really, to go up that first time alone, but I have devised a plan to take the biggest bite out of it and put the biggest shot of pleasure into it. The key to my plan is to check the weather carefully. It may take several attempts to get all the factors right, but it will be worth it.

What the beginning IFR pilot needs is to plan a trip to a destination that is extremely good VFR—preferably scattered clouds or clear. The origination point needs to be IFR; 500 feet to 1,000 feet would be excellent. The layers shouldn't be too thick. The idea is to climb out and get used to the feeling of being in the clouds on your own. All the time you should be calmed by the fact that you are flying towards improving weather. This first taste is so important and builds confidence.

Upon arriving at the other end, check weather and make sure the destination at home is going to be the same as when you left or will be improving. Incidentally, this should be one of the prerequisites for making the flight in the beginning. Then file back and try the approach. In 500 and 3 weather or better there is no pressure. It will be easier than training.

The next time out, look for relatively close conditions that are IFR, but where the origination point is impeccable VFR. Carry enough fuel to return to the VFR conditions in case things go bad at the planned destination. Shoot for 500 and 2 miles weather conditions. A good approach to an airport in those conditions is great for confidence. The trip back should be a snap, but don't forget to check weather.

On the third attempt to build experience, go when the weather is IFR all over. Keep it comfortable, though; 800 to 500 foot ceilings should be the rule and one mile visibility for the attempt. This trip will break the ice for good and send you well on the way down the road of experience.

WE'VE COME A LONG WAY

Although nostalgia occasionally creeps up on us, few of us true instrument pilots would trade the convenience and utility of today's planes if it came right down to it. The old birds are unique and hold a special and revered place in aviation. There is nothing quite like strolling around an old grass airport and peering through cobwebs

Fig. 8-2. And there are just some days ......

into musky smelling hangars. Those old biplanes with finely-stitched wings, delightfully perched on dainty, spoked wheels seem to invite a pilot to fly. And who of us would not enjoy it?

The trouble is that melon-sized gyros, leather helmets, and white scarves provide little in the way of business flying or the most utility we can squeeze out the airplane for every dollar we spend. The air vehicle of today is a dependable, sleek, all metal and finely upholstered plane. The instruments are not haphazardly thrown into the panel in any hole that fits. They are thoughtfully arranged in what we now refer to as the basic "T". Scanning during instrument conditions is not as much an art as it used to be. The "T" arrangement lends itself to quick methodical scanning. As a result, most pilots have a very similar scan.

Radios are solid state as opposed to the old tubes. No more do we crank in a signal like we were trying to separate the cream from the milk. In the past three years, I have noticed a definite upgrading in signal quality coming from most general aviation planes. This makes long hours of listening to center and approach frequencies easier.

In general things are better and should continue to be so. In order to keep pace with technological advances, the pilot must always take his flying seriously and familiarize himself with the new literature that continually flows from the magazines and books such as this one. Actually, a great deal of experience can be supplemented by reading.

There are no armchair ways to learn to fly instruments like a professional (Fig. 8-2). It is going to take a certain amount of "doing." The prudent pilot will learn or extract the most from each of his experiences in order that the bad ones and close calls will never be repeated.

As I said before, the satisfaction in watching one's own experience level grow with each flight can be appreciated by any pilot.

Glossary

Glossary

Additional services—Advisory information provided by ATC which includes, but is not limited to, the following:

- ☐ Traffic advisories
- ☐ Vectors, when requested by the pilot, to assist aircraft receiving traffic advisories to avoid observed
- ☐ Altitude deviation information of 300 feet or more.
- ☐ Advisories that traffic is no longer a factor
- ☐ Weather and chaff information
- ☐ Weather assistance
- ☐ Bird activity information
- ☐ Holding pattern surveillance

Additional services are provided to the extent possible contingent only upon the controller's capability to fit them into the performance of higher priority duties and on the basis of limitations of the radar, volume of traffic, frequency congestion and controller workload. The controller has complete discretion for determining if he is able to provide a service in a particular case. The controller's reason not to provide or continue to provide a service in a particular instance is *not* subject to question by the pilot and need not be made known to him.

(In non-mandatory radar service areas where a pilot feels he is getting unnecessary vectors, he can cancel ATC service as well. In this case the pilot need not tell the controller the reason. As you can see, it is a two-way street.)

Airmet/Airman's meteorological information—Inflight weather advisories which cover moderate icing, moderate turbulence, sustained winds of 30 knots or more within 2,000 feet of the surface, and the initial onset of phenomena producing extensive areas of visibilities below three miles or ceiling less than 1,000 feet. It concerns weather phenomena which are of operational interest to all aircraft and potentially hazardous to aircraft having limited capability because of lack of equipment, instrumentation or pilot qualifications.

Automated Radar Terminal Systems/ARTS—The generic term for the ultimate in functional capability afforded by several automation systems. Each differs in functional capabilities and equipment. ARTS plus a suffix Roman numeral denotes a specific system. A following letter indicates a major modification to that system. In general, an ARTS displays for the terminal controller aircraft indentification, flight plan data, other flight associated information such as altitude and speed, and aircraft position symbols in conjunction with his radar presentation. Normal radar co-exists with the alphanumeric display. In addition to enhancing visualization of the air traffic situation, ARTS facilitate intra/interfacility transfer and coordination of flight information. These capabilities are enabled by specially designed computers and subsystems tailored to the radar and communications equipments and operational requirements of each automated facility. Modular design permits adoption of improvements in computer software and electronic technologies as they become available while retaining the characteristics unique to each system.

ARTS IA — The functional capabilities and equipment of the New Common IFR Room Terminal Automation System, it tracks primary as well as secondary targets derived from two radar sources. The aircraft targets are displayed on a radar-type console by means of an alphanumeric generator. Aircraft identity is depicted in association with the appropriate aircraft target. When the aircraft is equipped with an encoded altimeter, its altitude is also displayed. The system can exchange flight plan information with the ARTCC.

ARTS II — Programmable non-tracking computer-aided display subsystems capable of modular expansion, ARTS II systems provide a level of automated air traffic control capability at terminals having low to medium activity.

Flight identification and altitude may be associated with the display of secondary radar targets. Also, flight plan information may be exchanged between the terminal and ARTCC.

ARTS III — The Beacon Tracking Level (BTL) of the modular programmable automated radar terminal system in use at medium to high activity terminals, ARTS III detects tracks and predicts secondary radar-derived aircraft targets. These are displayed by means of computer generated symbols and alphanumeric characters depicting flight identification altitude, ground speed and flight plan data. Although it does not track primary targets, they are displayed coincident with the secondary radar as well as the symbols and alphanumerics. The system has the capability of communicating with ARTCC's and other ARTS III facilities. ARTS II is found at all Group II and III TCA's

ARTS IIIA — The Radar Tracking and Beacon Tracking Level of the modular programmable automated radar terminal system, ARTS IIIA detects, tracks and predicts primary as well as secondary radar-derived aircraft targets. An enhancement of the ARTS III, this more sophisticated computer-driven system will eventually replace the ARTS IA system and upgrade about half of the existing ARTS II systems. The enhanced system will provide improved tracking, continuous data recording and fail-safe capabilities.

Climb to VFR—ATC authorization for an aircraft to climb to VFR conditions within a control zone when the only weather limitation is restricted visibility. The aircraft must remain clear of clouds while climbing to VFR.

Pilots Automatic Telephone Weather Answering Service (PATWAS)—Recorded weather briefings are available at several locations. This service is called PATWAS. The recorded telephone briefing includes a weather forecast which emphasizes expected weather up to about 12 hours in advance. Forecasts given around 6 pm may be an 18-hour forecast, with emphasis on the outlook for the next morning. The PATWAS locations are found in Part 2 of the AIM under the FSS-CS/T Weather Service Telephone Numbers section.

Sigmet/significant meteorological information—A weather advisory issued concerning weather significant to the safety of all aircraft. SIGMET advisories cover tornadoes, lines of thunderstorms, embedded thunderstorms, large hail, severe and extreme turbulence, severe icing, and widespread dust or sandstorms that reduce visibility to less than three miles.

VFR not recommended—An advisory provided by a Flight Service Station to pilots during a preflight or inflight briefing that flight under Visual Flight Rules is not recommended. To be given when the current and forecasted weather conditions are at or below VFR minimums, it does not abrogate the pilot's authority to make his own decision.

Wind Shear—A change in wind speed and /or wind direction in a short distance, resulting in a tearing or shearing effect, it can exist in horizontal or vertical or, occasionally, in both directions.

Index

Index